Official Languages

- English
- Spanish
- French
- Dutch

ATLANTIC OCEAN

ma Islands

aco

hera

San Salvador
Rum Cay

Turks & Caicos

Virgin Islands

Anguilla

St. Maarten/St. Martin

Dominican Republic

Puerto Rico

Saba

Haiti

Antigua

Guadeloupe

Dominica

Martinique

IBBEAN SEA

St. Lucia

St. Vincent & the Grenadines

Barbados

Grenada

Aruba

Curacao

Los Roques

Margarita Is.

Tobago

Bonaire

Cubagua

Trinidad

Venezuela

Guyana

Colombia

REEF CORAL
Identification

FLORIDA CARIBBEAN BAHAMAS
Including Marine Plants

PAUL HUMANN
NED DELOACH

NEW WORLD PUBLICATIONS, INC.

Jacksonville, Florida USA

Acknowledgements

This book was the result of considerable encouragement, help, and advice from many friends and acquaintances. It became a much larger undertaking and involved many more people than ever expected. The authors wish to express their sincere gratitude to everyone involved. Naturally, the names of a few who played especially significant roles come to mind.

Mary DeLoach, Nancy DeLoach and Jackie Jones gave valuable assistance in the editing process. Joe Gies and Michael O'Connell were most helpful with advice and assistance in design, layout, typesetting and production.

Long time friend Adrien Briggs, and the entire staff at Sunset House, Grand Cayman helped make our photographic trip to the islands most successful. Fellow underwater photographer Cathy Church and her staff kept our cameras working and provided important daily developing service. Diving companions Sol Fiser and Mike Bacon were indispensable assistants in finding many of the cryptic corals. Wonderful friends, John and Marion Bacon gave generously of their time, assistance, and boat, helping me photograph corals of East Florida. Captain Dan Morrison, Captain Julie Jordan and Jason Wesley of the Aggressor Fleet offered valuable assistance in finding uncommon species. Mark Ulmann's knowledge of northeast Florida's reefs was most valuable. Peter Hull and Gary Gilliland with Mote Marine Laboratory, in Sarasota, Florida, expedited our locating and photographing several species unique to West Florida.

PHOTO CREDITS

Mike Bacon, 193m, 195t, 213t, 215t, 226m; *Dr. Andrew Bruckner,* 241b, 243m&b, 245m&b, 247tm&b, 248br, 249t&b, 250b, 251tm&b, 252b, 253t&b, 254br, 255b, 256b, 257t&m, 261t&mr, 263ml,bl&r, 265t&m, 267b, 268b, 269t; *Jeri Clark,* 118tl; *Ned DeLoach,* 72m, 73t, 76b, 77m &b, 78 m & b, 79 t, m &b, 102m, 103t &m, 190 m, 255t, 259t, 273t &bl, 275b; *Dr. Walter Jaap,* 91b; *Doug Perrine,* 274tl, tr & b, 275m; *Graeme Teague,* 273br, 275t; *Dr. Ernesto Weil,* 107b, 109b, 135t; the remaining 485 pictures were taken by **Paul Humann**.

CREDITS

Photography Editor: Eric Riesch
Art Direction & Illustrations: Michael O'Connell
Print Consultant: D2Print, Singapore
First Edition: 1992
Second Edition, First Printing 2002; Second Printing 2003, Third Printing 2006.
ISBN 1-878348-32-9
First Edition Copyright, ©1992, Second Edition Copyright, ©2002 by Paul Humann
All rights reserved. No part of this book may be reproduced without prior written consent.
Published and Distributed by New World Publications, Inc., 1861 Cornell Road, Jacksonville, FL 32207,
Phone (904) 737-6558

Scientific Acknowledgements

Special tribute must be given to the numerous scientists who gave freely of their time, advice and knowledge. Each is a preeminent authority in their respective field, and without their most generous assistance, this book could have never been published. Every attempt was made to keep the text and identifications accurate. Where errors may exist, they are the authors' sole responsibility.

First Edition

The invaluable assistance of **Dr. Walter Goldberg,** of Florida International University, deserves special mention. He undertook the Herculean task as principal scientific advisor, and coordinator for this project. **Dr. Dennis Opresko** with the Oak Ridge National Laboratory assisted with black corals. **Dr. Dale Calder** from the Royal Ontario Museum offered advice on the fire corals. **Dr. David Ballantine,** Department of Marine Sciences, University of Puerto Rico advised and identified algae.

Dr. Stephen Cairns with the National Museum of Natural History, Smithsonian Institution was our primary mentor for stony corals. To substantiate the identifications of many species, small samples were collected of many photographed specimens and shipped to the Smithsonian for his examination. Those specimens were placed in the permanent National Collection and are indicated in this book by their "USNM" numbers. **Dr. Walter Jaap** with the Florida Marine Research Institute also assisted with stony corals, examining and identifying several collected specimens. **Dr. Douglas Fenner,** Australian Institute of Marine Science, has been a constant source of valuable information. He located a number of uncommon species, provided several pictures and was especially helpful in sorting out visual ID clues to similar appearing Agaricia species.

Dr. Jennifer Wheaton with the Florida Marine Research Institute was our primary advisor for octocorallians. Her knowledge from reef survey work was invaluable in establishing visual identification keys for many species. Dr. Goldberg made several dives with me to help sort out the mind boggling variety of octocorallians off Florida's east coast. In the laboratory he taught me how scientists reduce small slivers of gorgonian specimens to their structural spicules to determine their species by microscopic examination. Several difficult identification problems were forwarded to **Dr. Frederick Bayer,** the acknowledged world's octocorallian authority at the Smithsonian. Because of his help, the photographs of several living species were published in this book for the first time.

Second Edition

Dr. Stephen Cairns continues in this edition as our primary advisor for stony corals. Coral researcher **Deborah Danaher, MS,** scrutinized the stony coral text for scientific errors, changes in taxonomic nomenclature and assisted in making appropriate text revisions. She also helped to compile Appendix III: *The Reproduction and Growth of Stony Corals.* **Dr. Judith Lang,** an independent coral researcher, and **Dr. Ernesto Weil,** Department of Marine Sciences, University of Puerto Rico, provided invaluable lists of suggestions and changes.

It is common knowledge that coral reefs around the world are in a state of decline. Consequently, recognizing and monitoring these changes is of paramount importance. **Dr. Andrew Bruckner,** a Coral Reef Ecologist specializing in coral diseases and predation, associated with the Office of Protected Resources, NOAA/National Marine Fisheries Service, graciously volunteered to compile the text and provide photographic documentation for Appendix II: *Coral Health and Mortality.* It is our hope that this timely addition will serve as a useful guide for scientists, as well as concerned recreational divers, monitoring the health of the tropical western Atlantic coral reefs.

About the Authors

Paul Humann & Ned DeLoach

To find Paul Humann at his south Florida home, you have to cut through his dining room, which is lined with primitive art from jungle civilizations around the world. The large family room, no less impressively decorated, showcases fish, turtle and whale carvings – each the creation of island hands. A splendid collection of his favorite Galapagos wildlife prints covers the left wall; a dozen fiercely proud New Guinea tribesmen stare down from their tack-sharp portraits on the wall just to the right of the back door. Outside, a wooden deck, perpetually shaded by a towering mango tree, curves to the right under spreading limbs dripping with fern and orchid baskets, passes through a jungle of Australia tree ferns and bromeliads, and ends abruptly before a nondescript aluminum storm door that opens into the unkempt garage/office of an extremely busy man.

Whenever Paul has been in the States during the past 22 years, he has spent most of his time here. Early mornings to late evenings find him wedged in a pre-1970 K-Mart swivel chair that sits hopelessly trapped by fallen reams of drafts, correspondence and scientific publications before the tireless glow of a computer screen. Steam from a stained mug filled with strong Ecuadorian brew spirals up from the clutter. On the unfinished plyboard table to his left are two color-corrected slide viewing boxes, spread with an ocean of blue transparencies, illuminating book shelves packed with a well-used marine life library. From a nail hangs a cheaply framed Juris Doctor degree – a relic from an almost forgotten time. The remainder of the 10 X 29 foot concrete floor supports cheap, metal shelving piled with various office supplies, darkroom equipment and an unplanned museum of underwater photography equipment. A few dust covered pieces date from mid-century – the embryonic era of underwater exploration. The only order found anywhere occurs behind the thick, double doors of a large fire safe where carefully labeled and neatly stacked transparency storage cases hold treasures from 40 years of bountiful underwater hunting with a camera.

Though Paul's photographic search for marine species started in the 1960's, it really began in earnest in 1971 when he left a successful law practice in his hometown Wichita, Kansas to buy and captain the now legendary *Cayman Diver:* the Caribbean's first successful live-aboard diving cruiser. This bold move offered the unique opportunity to dive daily with the exotic creatures of the Caribbean reef. Paul sold the yacht in 1979, gaining even more freedom to travel, write and explore the world's coral reefs.

Hard work, continuous study and the courage to follow his dream, have led to the publication of 14 books, numerous magazine articles and a three volume *Reef Set.* Paul's pioneering efforts in marine life identification have required much more than capturing each species on film.

Collection, preservation and shipment of photographed specimens to scientific mentors around the world were required to establish identifications for hundreds of species.

Even with all his accomplishments, Paul has no intention of resting on past achievements. He continues to write and teach about marine life and gather information and photographs for future editions of the *Reef Set*. He does, however, plan to spend less time in his office and more time where he loves to be – traveling the world.

After finishing a degree in education in 1967 Ned DeLoach moved from his childhood home in west Texas to Florida so that he would be able to do what he loves best – dive. In 1971 he completed his first diving guide to the state, *Diving Guide to Underwater Florida*, which was released in its 11th edition in 2004. In the mid-1970s Ned and Paul co-edited *Ocean Realm* magazine. It was during this period that the idea of a marine life identification series designed for divers was born. In 1989, the 1st edition of *Reef Fish Identification* was published by New World Publications, Inc., their jointly owned marine life education publishing house. Beginning in 1995 Ned and his wife Anna spent five consecutive summers in Bimini, Bahamas researching fish behavior for the book *Reef Fish Behavior* written in collaboration with Paul and published in 2000. Ned and Anna live in Jacksonville, Florida.

Authors' Note

Corals flourish in warm, clear, shallow seas. Along the Florida Keys' Atlantic fringe, throughout the Bahama Island chain, and spreading south and west across the tropical water of the Caribbean Sea, great coral reefs proliferate. Towering sea-sculptures adorned with waving gardens of flexible coral fans, whips and plumes provide sanctuary to one of the Earth's most diverse and visually stunning ecosystems.

It has only been with our recent ability to freely explore this dramatic underwater wilderness that we are beginning to unravel its complex nature. Even with limited data, it is readily apparent that environmental changes both natural and manmade have had a harsh impact on coral habitats. Coastal development, oil spills, overharvesting, groundings, global warming, El Niño, algal blooms and storms: the list of culprits is long. Our lack of knowledge, however, is the reef's greatest threat.

An ancient Chinese proverb states: THE BEGINNING OF WISDOM IS GETTING THINGS BY THEIR RIGHT NAME. A single, healthy reef section may consist of over 50 coral species, but only a few divers are able to identify even the most common corals. The ability to recognize individual life forms on the reef is the critical distinction between an underwater sightseer and the underwater naturalist.

The guardianship of the world's coral gardens should, by right, be led by the recreational diving community. For decades bird watchers have been accumulating a wealth of data by monitoring bird populations. Their enjoyable pastime has produced an invaluable resource for their environmental concerns. Comparable information about the reef's inhabitants remains unavailable even for areas that are visited by thousands of divers each year. It seems sensible that recreational divers should make a similar commitment to marine life by taking an active role monitoring our coral reefs.

Reef Coral Identification is the first comprehensive photographic guide for the visual identification of corals and marine plants that inhabit the Florida, Caribbean and Bahaman waters. It is designed to help underwater naturalists as well as scientists, distinguish the many species of coral, algae and coral diseases encountered while exploring the reefs. *Reef Coral Identification, 2nd edition*, is the third text of the three-volume *Reef Set* that includes *Reef Fish Identification, 3rd edition*, and *Reef Creature Identification, 2nd edition*.

Contents

Ten Identification Groups
Common & Proper Phylum Names

1. Hydrocorals   14-21

Fire Corals   Lace Coral

2. Gorgonians   22-85

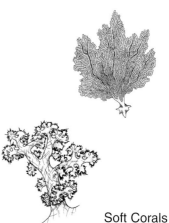

Typical Shapes
of Gorgonians

Telestaceans   Soft Corals

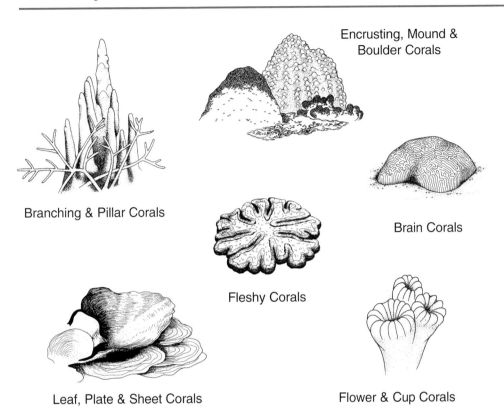

Encrusting, Mound &
Boulder Corals

Branching & Pillar Corals

Brain Corals

Fleshy Corals

Leaf, Plate & Sheet Corals

Flower & Cup Corals

4. Black Corals 176-187

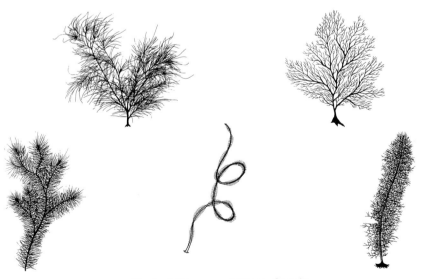

Typical Shapes of Black Corals

Overview

Corals are tiny animals that generally group together by the thousands, forming colonies that attach to hard surfaces of the sea floor. By drawing calcium carbonate from seawater they build skeletal structures in an infinite variety of shapes and sizes. Those species known as reef building corals, produce massive skeletons that collectively form the limestone framework of tropical reefs. Throughout the ages a vast array of animals and plants have become associated with coral reefs, creating some of our earth's most fascinating, complex and biologically diverse ecosystems.

All corals are members of the Animal Kingdom and classified in Phylum Cnidaria (Nigh-DARE-ee-uh/ L. a nettle [formerly known as Phylum Coelenterata/L. open gut]). They are often mistaken for plants because of their attachment to the substrate, apparent lack of independent movement and superficial resemblance to flora. In fact, corals were classified as plants until 1753, when French biologist J.A. de Peysonell, making a study in the western Atlantic, concluded they were animals. Although corals are the best known cnidarians, the phylum also includes several other well-known groups including hydroids, jellyfish, and anemones.

Cnidarians have a simple anatomy consisting of a cup-shaped body, with a single, central opening that is encircled by tentacles. This opening functions both as a mouth and anus. Most phylum members attach their bodies to the substrate; in this form they are known as polyps. Polyps can live singly, such as most anemones, or they can reproduce asexually to form ever expanding colonies, which is typical of most corals. Noncolonial, unattached, free swimming members of the phylum are known as medusa or jellyfish. A unique characteristic shared by virtually all cnidarians is the presence of numerous stinging capsules, called nematocysts or cnidae, which is the origin of the phylum's Latin name. These minute capsules, located primarily on the tentacles, are used for both capturing prey and defense. With the exception of fire corals, the stings of most corals have no harmful effect on divers.

For coral reefs to develop, the delicate polyps must flourish. This requires several critical environmental factors, including: water temperature, movement, salinity, clarity, and a firm base for attachment. Water temperature must generally remain between 70 and 85 degrees Fahrenheit for the reef building colonies to grow. Species can survive below or above these points, but do not grow at a rate sufficient to construct reefs. Water movement sustains life by refreshing the supply of planktonic food and oxygen. Water clarity is also important. It allows the passage of light, essential for the growth of single-celled plants, called zooxanthellae (zo-zan-THEL-ee), that grow within the coral polyps' tissue. Zooxanthellae play a vital role in the polyps' ability to produce calcium carbonate for their skeletons. Reduced clarity, caused by settling silt particles, limits the polyps' ability to feed by literally choking them. Even under ideal conditions coral growth is slow, measuring less than an inch each year for most species.

In addition to the reef building corals this volume also includes the cnidarians commonly known as fire corals, lace corals, gorgonians (sometimes called soft corals) and black corals. All other cnidarians are identified in the companion volume, *Reef Creature Identification*. Marine flowering plants and algae play a vital role in the reefs' ecosystems and are included in Appendix I. Many of these species, known as coralline algae, also employ calcium carbonate to support their structure. In this way they contribute substantially to the reef building process by filling voids and actually cementing the reef's framework together. Appendix II – *Coral Health and Mortality* is a timely addition to the 2nd edition because of the proliferation in the past decade of diseases affecting corals throughout the region. In many areas the majority of shallow-water branching coral gardens have been lost to disease infections for yet undetermined reasons. Hopefully, this review will serve as a standard resource for groups and individuals monitoring the spread and affects of coral diseases so that we can better understand the causes and dynamics of this daunting phenomenon. Appendix III – *The Reproduction and Growth of Stony Corals* present a delightful pictorial essay of one of natures most majestic procreations: the annual mass spawning of stony corals.

Types of Coral Reefs, Structures and Terms

The basic types of coral reefs are generally defined by their overall structure and the geological conditions under which they evolved. These distinctions are sometimes obscure because of overlapping stages in the continuum of their development. Most marine scientists agree that there are three basic types of coral reefs and possibly five. In broad, idealized terms, the reef types may be described as follows:

Fringing Reefs grow out from the shore or are separated by a shallow lagoon. They generally parallel the coastline and at their shallowest often break or nearly reach the water's surface. They are common around most Caribbean and Bahamian islands, but are virtually absent along both Florida coasts and the Florida Keys. Geologically they are considered to be the youngest type of reef.

Barrier Reefs generally grow parallel to a coastline, but are separated by extensive distance and a relatively deep lagoon. The distance may vary from about one mile to 25 miles or more and the lagoon often exceeds 60 feet in depth. At their shallowest they often break or nearly reach the water's surface, forming a "barrier" to navigation. The outer edge of a barrier reef drops from the island platform or continental shelf into very deep water. The best example in the Western Hemisphere is the world's second longest, skirting the small Central American country of Belize. Typically, fringing reefs change to barrier reefs when their associated land mass undergoes a slow geologic sinking.

Atolls are open sea reefs that form rings, ovals or horseshoe-shapes around a shallow lagoon. Occasionally small coral islands that may support vegetation form as a part of the ring. On the outside the fore reef drops into deep water. Atolls are generally found in the tropical Pacific where large geological plates supporting volcanic peaks gradually sink. Fringing reefs first form around the volcanic islands. As the plate sinks, the reefs become more distant from the land and grow upward, forming barrier reefs. The final stage of an atoll's development occurs when the volcanic island is completely submerged, leaving the lagoon in its place. There are a few atolls in the Western Atlantic, but they were not formed from submerging volcanos as in the Pacific. The best known are Lighthouse, Glovers' and Turneffe off Belize, Chinchirro off Yucatan and Hogsty in the Bahamas.

Bank Reefs are open sea reefs, without a central lagoon, surrounded by deep water and miles from any land mass. The Great Bahama Bank, Ten Mile Banks off Grand Cayman, and Serranilla Bank and Misteriosa Bank located in the Northwest Caribbean are well-known examples. Some scientists also describe the reefs off the Florida Keys as bank reefs, while others consider them as a combination of bank and barrier.

Patch Reefs are small, isolated reef areas that grow up from the open bottom of the island platform or continental shelf. They generally occur between the fringing reefs and barrier reef, if one is present. A patch reef may vary in size from a small house to an area that could cover several city blocks. Depths also vary greatly, but the reef's crest rarely breaks the surface.

Coral Heads are similar to patch reefs, but smaller in size. They are primarily formed by a single coral colony, such as a huge brain or star coral, but may include several smaller colonies of the same or different species.

Reef Crest is the top of a reef system.

Back Reef is the area behind fringing reefs, usually protected, calm and often containing a mosaic of shallow coral heads, patch reefs and turtle grass.

Lagoon is a relatively shallow, calm, protected area behind a fringing or barrier reef. It often includes great expanses of sand flats and grass beds and occasional coral heads.

Fore Reef is the area on the seaward side of any reef, but refers primarily to the portions that project into deeper water.

Tongue & Groove are long ridges separated by valleys of sand that generally run toward the direction of the prevailing swells. They often occur in shallow water near the reef crests, but may also be found on the fore reef. The ridges are also termed spurs or buttresses. The valleys are also called sand channels, sand chutes, and, if narrow with high, steep sides, canyons.

Walls are underwater cliffs that drop at or near a 90 degree angle. They are often associated with the outer limits of an island platform or continental shelf.

Wall Lips are ridges that often form and run along the upper edge of a wall. The ridge can be slight or over 20 to 30 feet in height.

How to Use This Book

The animals in Phylum Cnidaria are classified further by scientists into class, order, family, genus and species. Similar appearing Cnidarians, commonly recognized by the public as a group, such as fire corals, stony corals, black corals, etc., usually fall completely within one of the lower classifications. These **Commonly Recognized Groups** are important reference keys for using this text. The predominant anatomical features that distinguish each of the eleven groups included are summarized in their corresponding Identification Group introduction. Stony corals, because of their large number, are further divided into six structural/appearance groups. All groups are also listed with a visual reference diagram under their associated group in the contents pages, in the quick reference index on the inside back cover, at the top of the left page where their members are described in the text, and in bold type next to the identification photograph. It is important, as a first step in coral identification, to become familiar with these groups and their locations within the text.

Names

Information about each species begins with the animal's common name (that used by the general public). Using common names for identification of corals by scientists is impractical because several species are known by more than one name. For example, Grooved Brain Coral, *Diploria labyrinthiformis,* is also commonly known as Depressed Brain Coral, Labyrinthine Brain Coral and just plain Brain Coral. The common names used in this text are based on previously published names. If more than one name has been published, the one most commonly used or the name which best incorporates an anatomical feature that would help the layman remember and recognize the species was selected. Previously published common names are listed in a "NOTE" at the end of the text describing each species. Several species included have never had a common name published. In these instances, a name was selected that describes a distinctive feature that can be used for visual identification. It is hoped that the common names used in this text will become standardized so future confusion will be eliminated. In this book common species names are capitalized to help set them apart, although this practice is not considered grammatically correct.

Below the common name, in italics, is the two-part scientific name. The first word (always capitalized) is the genus. The genus name is given to a group of animals with very similar physiological characteristics. The second word (never capitalized) is species. A species includes only animals that are sexually compatible and produce fertile offspring. Occasionally "sp." appears in the place of a species name, this means the species is not known. If a "n." proceeds the "sp." it means it is a new, scientifically undescribed species. Continuing below genus and species, in descending order, is a list of classification categories to which the genus and species belong. This scientific nomenclature, rooted in Latin (L.) and Greek (Gr.) is used by scientists throughout the world.

Size

The average size range of the species divers are most likely to observe. Occasionally, the diameter of coral cups, branches, etc. is also given if this information may be useful in visual identification.

Depth

The reported depth range in scientific literature, although species are occasionally found outside these limits. The depths at which a species is most commonly found is given in HABITAT & BEHAVIOR. Depths below the recommended safe diving limit of 130 feet are given only as a matter of scientific interest. Species that live exclusively below 130 feet are not included.

Visual ID

Colors, markings, and anatomical differences that distinguish the species from similar appearing species. In most cases, these features are readily apparent to divers, but occasionally they are quite subtle. Generally the coral's colonial structure is described first, followed by distinguishing characteristics, and finally colors. If the colonial structure of the species is fragile, this information is also included in this section.

Abundance & Distribution

Abundance refers to a diver's likelihood of observing a species in its normal habitat and depth range on any given dive. This is not necessarily indicative of the actual populations. Definitions are as follows:

Abundant - At least several sightings can be expected on nearly every dive.

Common - Sightings are frequent, but not necessarily on every dive.

Occasional - Sightings are not unusual, but not on a regular basis.

Uncommon - Sightings are unusual.

Rare - Sightings are exceptional.

Distribution describes where the species may be found geographically within the range of the map on the opposite page. The Turks and Caicos Islands are included as an extension of the Bahama Island chain. Described species may also be found in areas such as Bermuda and Brazil, but no attempt has been made to include this specific information in every identification, although additional data has occasionally been included. In many instances the extent of a species' geographical range is not yet known; consequently, species may occasionally be found in areas not listed. If sightings are made that do not correspond with the geographic information provided, the publisher is interested in obtaining details for updating future editions.

Habitat & Behavior

Habitat is the type of underwater terrain where a particular species is likely to be found. Habitats frequented by divers, such as natural and artificial reefs, adjacent areas of sand and rubble, sea grass beds and walls are emphasized.

Behavior is the animal's normal activities that can be observed by a diver and used in identification.

Effect On Divers

If a species is known to have a negative effect on divers, it is listed. The agent of the injury, how it might occur, symptoms, and recommended treatment are included where appropriate.

Similar Species

Occasionally there are similar appearing species that are not pictured. Generally they are corals and marine plants that for one reason or another are rarely observed. Characteristics and information are given that identify and distinguish them from the species pictured.

Note

Additional information that may help in the visual identification process such as: recent changes in classification and nomenclature, other common names also used for the same species, or details relating to the method used to identify the photographed specimen. Several photographed specimens are now part of the National Collection at the Smithsonian. Their catalog numbers (USNM) may also appear next to the specimen's photograph.

Authors' Note on Taxonomy

Biological scientists that specialize in identifying, describing and classifying plants and animals according to their presumed natural relationships, are called taxonomists. Generally they are a rare breed because of the limited research money and grants and few positions available in museums and universities for their particular talents. In fact, for many world authorities taxonomy is more a hobby than a profession. Their job descriptions generally entail other studies such as biomedical research, reef surveys, commercial marine harvesting, ecological and environmental surveys, etc. One of our most pressing problems during the extended research for each volume of the Reef Set was finding taxonomists to help with the identification process. For instance, it was necessary to correspond with a retired scientist from the British Museum of Natural History to acquire information concerning flatworms for the *Reef Creature* text — there was no one in the United States who could help!

Biological research is based on accurate taxonomy, yet lack of funding for this discipline continues to be a problem. A recent example came to light in a 1992 paper by Nancy Knowlton, *et al,* who found evidence that Boulder Star Coral [pg. 113] commonly used as an indicator of reef health is probably four closely related but separate species with different growth rates and reactions to changes. If her findings are correct, it means that the conclusions drawn from years of ecological and environmental reef research in Florida, the Bahamas and Caribbean may be invalid! The need for more basic taxonomy research is further emphasized by the eight scientifically undescribed species included in this book, not to mention the even larger number of described species that desperately need further study and possible reclassification.

There is general scientific agreement on the organization of corals from Family through the genus levels of scientific taxonomy. However, at the species level, classification occasionally becomes blurred. For example, two corals with identical corallites growing in different environments may differ in their growth patterns: one specimen may have thick branches while another specimen produces substantially thinner branches. To determine if the specimens are a single species or represent two different species entirely, it is necessary to determine if the growth variations are the product of a species' genetic makeup, or the result of differing conditions where each specimen originated. Coral taxonomists are working continually to answer such questions; however, the process in differentiating between closely related species is a difficult and, often an inexact process requiring examination by highly trained individuals using sophisticated scientific techniques. At the species level, we have attempted in this text to reflect the majority opinion of researchers currently working in the field, and to note where controversies exist.

IDENTIFICATION GROUP 1

Class Hydrozoa
(High-druh-ZO-uh / Gr. water animal)
Hydrocorals

Hydrocorals are hydroid colonies that secrete hard, calcareous skeletons. They are often thought to be stony corals, but the resemblance is superficial. There are two types, fire and lace corals.

Fire Corals

Family Milleporidae (Mill-LEE-pore-ih-dee / L. thousand pores)

Fire coral, or stinging coral as it is sometimes called, often produces a painful burning sensation when touched by bare skin. The pain is usually short-lived and neither severe or dangerous. For a few sensitive individuals, however, it can cause redness, welts and a rash that can last for several days. This reaction is caused by unusually powerful **batteries of stinging nematocysts** on the tentacles of the tiny polyps.

In the event of a sting, never rub the affected area or wash with fresh water or soap. Both actions can cause untriggered nematocysts to discharge. Saturating the affected area with vinegar immobilizes unspent nematocysts; a sprinkling of meat tenderizer may also help alleviate the symptoms.

The hard, calcareous skeleton of fire coral appears relatively smooth. Close observation, however, reveals a fuzzy covering which is actually the colony's tiny, hair-like polyps extending through thousands of **pinhole-sized pores**. There are two types of polyps, **sensory/stinging (dactylozooids)** and **feeding (gastrozooids).** The feeding polyps are stout and encircled by five to nine, tall, thin sensory/stinging polyps. The polyp's gastric cavities are interconnected beneath the skeletal surface. Fire corals are generally tan to mustard with white at the tips or edges of the skeletal structure.

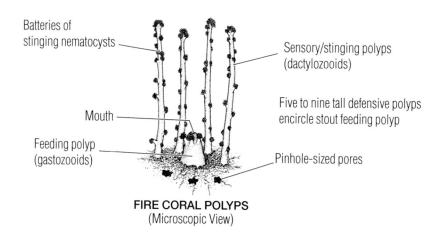

Batteries of stinging nematocysts

Sensory/stinging polyps (dactylozooids)

Five to nine tall defensive polyps encircle stout feeding polyp

Mouth

Feeding polyp (gastozooids)

Pinhole-sized pores

FIRE CORAL POLYPS
(Microscopic View)

There are three growth patterns in the Caribbean — **branching, blade** and **box;** all often encrust. Most scientists believe these represent three distinct species. Some contend, however, that each is simply a growth form of the same species.

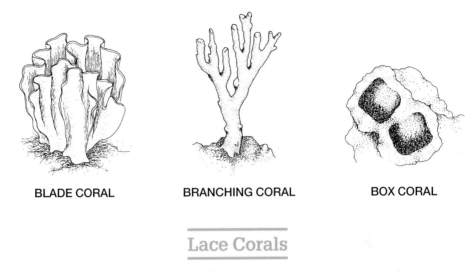

BLADE CORAL   BRANCHING CORAL   BOX CORAL

Lace Corals

Family Stylasteridae (Sty-LASS-ter-ih-dee / Gr. a pillar, and a star)

The common name "lace coral" is derived from their profusely branched, hard, calcareous skeleton. Like fire corals, lace corals have both sensory/stinging polyps (dactylozooids) and feeding polyps (gastrozooids). Stout feeding polyps are encircled by five to fifteen, tall, thin sensory/stinging polyps.

The polyps extend through pores in the calcareous skeleton and form small cup-like structures, similar in appearance to those of stony corals. These tiny cups give outer branches a **serrated appearance.** Occasional cups are also visible on the branches' thick bases. The polyp's gastric cavities are interconnected beneath the skeletal surface. Polyps have translucent hair-like appearance when extended. Small, hemispherical bumps occasionally grow on branches. Lace corals are usually shades of purple, burgundy or lavender at the base, fading to pink and white toward the branches' tips. There is only one species in the Caribbean.

Unlike fire corals, lace corals lack the powerful batteries of stinging nematocysts. They are not generally considered toxic to divers, although they can irritate sensitive skin.

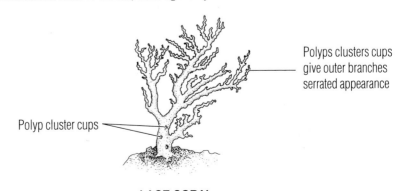

Polyps clusters cups give outer branches serrated appearance

Polyp cluster cups

LACE CORAL

VISUAL ID: Colonies form multiple branched structure. Branches generally cylindrical. Most commonly branch in a single plane, but occasionally in all directions. Often encrust and overgrow gorgonian colonies, taking on their shape. Surface texture smooth with numerous pin-hole size pores. When the tiny polyps protrude, they appear as short, fine hair. Tan to mustard and brown; branch tips white.

ABUNDANCE & DISTRIBUTION: Abundant to common Florida, Bahamas, Caribbean.

HABITAT & BEHAVIOR: Inhabit all marine environments. The only one of the three fire corals that commonly grows deeper than 30 feet and is relatively uncommon in shallow surge zones.

EFFECT ON DIVERS: Toxic; contact with bare skin will produce an intense, but usually short-lived, sting. May cause minor redness, welts and rash.

Branching Fire Coral
Encrusting substrate.

Branching Fire Coral
Encrusting sea feather plume.

**BRANCHING
FIRE CORAL**
Millepora alcicornis
FAMILY:
Fire Corals
Milleporidae

SIZE: 1 -18 in.
DEPTH: 3 - 130 ft.

Branching Fire Coral
Hair-like polyp detail.

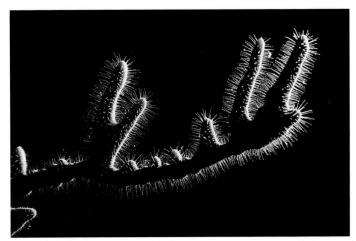

Branching Fire Coral
*Encrusting common
sea fan.*

VISUAL ID: Colonies form thin, upright blades or plates that extend from an encrusting base. Outer edge of blades uneven with multiple extensions or short branches. Surface texture smooth with numerous pin-hole size pores. When the tiny polyps protrude, they appear as short, fine hair. Tan to mustard and brown; blade edges white.

ABUNDANCE & DISTRIBUTION: Abundant to common Florida, Bahamas, Caribbean.

HABITAT & BEHAVIOR: Inhabit shallow water reef tops. Usually in areas with some water movement; most common in areas with constant surge.

EFFECT ON DIVERS: Toxic; contact with bare skin will produce an intense, but usually short-lived, sting. May cause minor redness, welts and rash.

Blade Fire Coral
Reef top colony.

VISUAL ID: Colonies form open-ended, thick-walled, box-like structures that extend upward from an encrusting base. Often join to form honeycomb pattern or encrust in rippled wave-like pattern. Surface texture smooth with numerous pin-hole size pores. When the tiny polyps protrude, they appear as short, fine hair. Tan to mustard brown, with reddish to pink or lavender tints that are distinctive of this species; open end edges of boxes whitish.

ABUNDANCE & DISTRIBUTION: Common to occasional Dominican Republic southward through Lesser Antilles to Brazil. Not reported Florida, Bahamas, North or West Caribbean.

HABITAT & BEHAVIOR: Inhabit shallow water reef tops. Usually in areas with some water movement, most common in areas with regular surge.

EFFECT ON DIVERS: Not considered toxic; although may sting sensitive skin.

**BLADE
FIRE CORAL**
Millepora complanata
FAMILY:
Fire Corals
Milleporidae

SIZE: 1 - 18 in.
DEPTH: 0 - 45 ft.

Blade Fire Coral
*Hair-like
polyp detail.*

BOX FIRE CORAL
Millepora squarrosa
FAMILY:
Fire Corals
Milleporidae

SIZE: ¹/₂ - 2 in.
DEPTH: 6 - 30 ft.

continued next page

VISUAL ID: Colonies form fan-like structures of branches. The cylindrical branches taper from base to tip. Tiny cups, formed by the feeding and the encircling stinging polyps, give outer branches a serrated appearance. Occasional cups also visible on branches' thick base. Polyps have translucent hair-like appearance when extended. Small, hemispherical bumps occasionally grow on branches. Purple to burgundy or lavender near colony base, fading to pink and white toward branch tips. Occasionally all white.

ABUNDANCE & DISTRIBUTION: Common South Florida, Bahamas, Caribbean.

HABITAT & BEHAVIOR: Inhabit protected, shaded areas of reefs. Often in cracks, under ledge overhangs, caves and recesses.

EFFECT ON DIVERS: Not considered toxic, although may sting sensitive bare skin.

Box Fire Coral
continued from previous page

Growth variations.

Stylaster roseus
FAMILY:
Lace Corals
Stylasteridae

SIZE: 1 - 4 in.
DEPTH: 15 - 100 ft.

Rose Lace Coral
Color variations.

Class Anthozoa

(An-thuh-ZO-uh / L. flower-like animal)

Subclass Octocorallia

(Octo-core-AL-ee-uh / Gr. & L. eight and coral animal)

Gorgonians, Telestaceans, Soft Corals

Octocorallian polyps have **eight tentacles** that bear tiny pinnate (feather-like) projections called **pinnules.** Octocoral colors come from one or a combination of three sources: pigments in the polyps' tissues; intracellular symbiotic algae in the polyps' tissues, called zooxanthellae (zo-zan-THEL-ee); and/or coloring minerals in the calcareous spicules of the colonial structure. Colors often vary between colonies of the same species and are rarely useful in the identification process. For those few species where color is a reliable identification characteristic, a dive light is necessary to reveal the true shade underwater. Occasionally, members of this subclass are inaccurately referred to as "horny corals" because their supporting skeletal material superficially resembles the horn-like protein of turtle shells, and the hoofs, horns, and antlers of mammals.

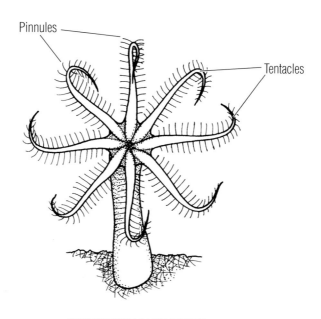

OCTOCORALLIAN POLYP

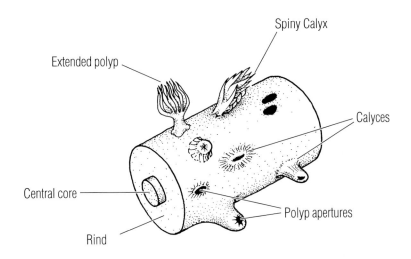

Extended polyp

Spiny Calyx

Calyces

Central core

Polyp apertures

Rind

GORGONIAN BRANCH
(Showing calyx and aperture variations)

Gorgonians

Traditionally **ORDER: Gorgonacea**

(Gore-GON-ace-ee-ah / Gr. ugly, terrible or myth of three sisters with snakes for hair)

SUBORDERS: Scleraxonia and Holaxonia

Gorgonians is the preferred name for this large group of octocorallians; however, they are commonly called "soft corals" because of the colonies' lack of a hard, rigid, permanent skeletons. The common name soft coral should be used when referring to members of the Family Nephtheidae, abundant in the Indo-Pacific. Gorgonians include the animal colonies known as sea rods, flat sea whips, sea feather plumes, sea fans and orange sea whips. To assist in visual identification, species have been arranged by the colony's shape and common name, rather than their traditional scientific grouping. In most instances this method keeps members of the same family and genus together.

The stems and branches of all gorgonians have a central skeleton or axis. The **central core** in the Suborder Scleraxonia is composed of either tightly bound or fused calcareous spicules. A wood-like core typifies the Suborder Holaxonia. The core is surrounded by gelatinous material called the **rind**. **Polyps** are embedded in the rind and extend their tentacles and bodies from surface openings (apertures). The arrangement of the polyps (in rows, alternating bands, randomly scattered, etc.) is often helpful in the identification process. The shape of **polyp apertures** and the rims around them, called **calyces (calyx, singular),** are often used to determine the genus and, occasionally, species.

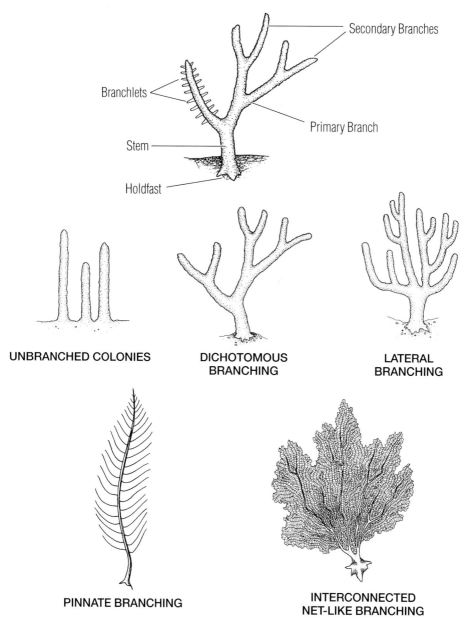

Secondary Branches

Branchlets

Primary Branch

Stem

Holdfast

UNBRANCHED COLONIES

DICHOTOMOUS BRANCHING

LATERAL BRANCHING

PINNATE BRANCHING

INTERCONNECTED NET-LIKE BRANCHING

Most gorgonian colonies are attached to the substrate by a single **holdfast** at the base of a stem that usually **branches.** This branching pattern, which includes **unbranched, dichotomous, lateral** and **pinnate branching** and **interconnected net-like branching,** is often characteristic of the genus and is occasionally distinctive in determining a species. Branching may be in a single plane or bushy. **Branchlets** are small, usually profuse, branches that in some species line the sides of the **primary branches.**

Unfortunately, less than half of the 60-70 reef gorgonians can be visually identified to species underwater. Positive identification requires microscopic examination of the location, pattern, shape and size of the skeletal spicules embedded in the polyp's and colony's common tissue.

Telestaceans

ORDER: Alcyonacea – SUBORDER: Stolonifera
FAMILY: Clavulariidae – SUBFAMILY: Telestinae
Traditionally **ORDER Telestacea** (Tell-uh-STAY-see-ah / Gr. poet)

Telestacean colonies grow by extending a long **terminal polyp** that produces a stem with short side branches tipped with **daughter polyps.** The polyps are brilliant white. They can often be identified by stem color, depth and geographical location. The stem's color, however, is frequently obscured by encrusting algae, sponge, and other organisms. Telestaceans are generally found in areas of moderate turbidity, and only rarely occur on clear water reefs. They are considered a fouling organism.

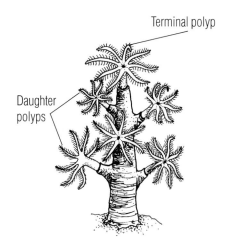

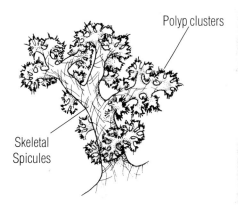

TELESTACEAN COLONY

SOFT CORAL COLONY

Soft Corals

ORDER: Alcyonacea (Al-see-uh-NAY-see-ah /Gr. a kingfisher)
FAMILY: Nephtheidae (NEF-the-ih-dee / Gr. lady of the house)

Soft corals resemble thick-trunked, branched trees. **Polyps** are clumped on the branch tips, and occasionally in small clusters and/or solitary polyps on the trunk or branches' surface. The pliable colony is composed of a rubbery or thick jelly-like material that is often translucent with the embedded **skeletal spicules** clearly visible. Colors are a wide range of pastel shades. Although profuse on Indo-Pacific reefs, there are only a few species in the tropical western Atlantic and these usually occur far below safe diving limits. On occasion, however, a few colonies may grow as shallow as 100 feet.

Gorgonians

VISUAL ID: Colonies form one to several erect, unbranched, cylindrical rods, arising from a common encrusting base. When extended, large polyps give colony "hairy" appearance. Area around pore-like polyp apertures often swollen. Rods (rind) violet to purple and purple-gray, occasionally with some tints of brown or tan; polyps greenish brown to brown and brownish gray. Colonies also form thick encrustations without any erect rod structures. Occasionally encrust branches of other gorgonians. (Compare similar appearing Encrusting Gorgonian, *Erythropodium caribaeorum*, [next] distinguished by tan rind and polyps.)

ABUNDANCE & DISTRIBUTION: Abundant to common South Florida, Bahamas, Caribbean.

HABITAT & BEHAVIOR: Inhabit most reef environments, especially shallow fringing, patch and back reef areas.

NOTE: Also commonly known as "Deadman's Fingers."

Corky Sea Finger

Comparison of colonies with polyps extended and retracted; note purplish shades of rind.

CORKY SEA FINGER
Briareum asbestinum
SUBORDER:
Scleraxonia
FAMILY:
Briareidae

SIZE: Colony height
$^1/_2$ - 24 in.
DEPTH: 3 - 100 ft.

Corky Sea Finger
*Colony encrusting
sea feather plume.*

Corky Sea Finger
*Comparison of polyps
extended and retracted.*

*Polyp detail;
encrusting variation.*
[far left]

Encrusting large area.
[left]

Gorgonians

VISUAL ID: Colonies form, encrusting mats. Extended polyps and tentacles appear as fine hair. When polyps retracted, rind appears smooth and leather-like, and apertures appear as pin-sized pores, rarely with slightly projecting calyces. Tan, underside reddish, apertures often whitish. (Similar encrusting variation of Corky Sea Fingers [previous] distinguished by thick, purplish rind and larger, darker polyps, often area around polyp apertures swollen.)

ABUNDANCE & DISTRIBUTION: Occasional Florida, Bahamas, Caribbean.

HABITAT & BEHAVIOR: Inhabit most reef environments, especially shallow fringing, patch and back reef areas.

Encrusting Gorgonian
Note fine, "hair-like" appearance of extended polyps.

VISUAL ID: Colonies are quite bushy, but grow in flat, vertical planes. Tend to branch laterally, with only occasional dichotomous branching. (Similar Bent Sea Rod [next] tends to branch dichotomously.) The contrast of light yellow-brown to brown polyps against dark brown to black stalks (rind) is a distinctive characteristic of this species. When polyps retracted, area around apertures is flat or protrudes only slightly.

ABUNDANCE & DISTRIBUTION: Common South Florida, Bahamas, Caribbean.

HABITAT & BEHAVIOR: Inhabit clear water patch reefs. Colonies growing in deeper water tend to have more slender branches in denser concentrations and grow taller than their shallow water counterparts.

ENCRUSTING GORGONIAN

Erythropodium caribaeorum

SUBORDER:
Scleraxonia
FAMILY:
Anthothelidae

SIZE: 3 in. - 3 ft.
DEPTH: 3 - 100 ft.

Encrusting Gorgonian

Comparison of extended and retracted polyps; note smooth texture of rind.

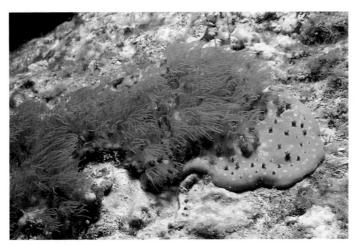

BLACK SEA ROD

Plexaura homomalla
SUBORDER:
Holaxonia
FAMILY:
Plexauridae

SIZE: Colony height
$^1/_2$ - 2 ft.
DEPTH: 4 - 200 ft.

continued next page 29

Gorgonians

Black Sea Rod
Branch detail with polyps retracted.

VISUAL ID: Colonies usually grow in flat, vertical planes with profuse dichotomous branching. (Similar Black Sea Rod [previous] tend to branch laterally.) Occasionally bushy, branching in all directions. Pale to tan, yellow-brown, brown, reddish purple and purple. Polyps occasionally lighter than stalk. When polyps retracted, rim of aperture is only slightly raised with a small lip or shelf around the inside.

ABUNDANCE & DISTRIBUTION: Common South Florida, Bahamas, Caribbean.

HABITAT & BEHAVIOR: Inhabit clear water patch reefs.

Bent Sea Rod
Branch detail with polyps retracted.

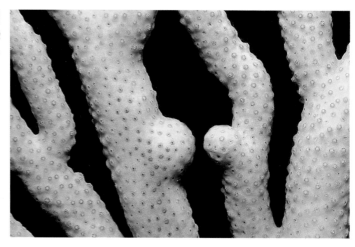

Black Sea Rod
continued from previous page

Small colony branch detail with polyps extended.

BENT SEA ROD
Plexaura flexuosa
SUBORDER:
Holaxonia
FAMILY:
Plexauridae

SIZE: Colony height
6 - 16 in.
DEPTH: 4 - 150 ft.

Bent Sea Rod
Branching in all directions.

Gorgonians

VISUAL ID: Sea rod colonies of this genus can be recognized when their polyps are retracted, leaving apertures that appear as round to oval pores without raised rims (calyces). All four species of this genus are so individually variable in appearance, and yet similar to one another, that they cannot easily be distinguished visually. Microscopic examination is required for positive identification. Colonies are generally bushy with stout stalks and branch dichotomously. Colors vary greatly from light brown to yellow-brown, brown, reddish purple, purple and gray.

ABUNDANCE & DISTRIBUTION: Common South Florida, Bahamas, Caribbean.

HABITAT & BEHAVIOR: Inhabit most clear water reef environments.

Porous Sea Rods
*Note pore-like polyp aperture
without raised calyces.*

POROUS SEA RODS
Pseudoplexaura spp.
SUBORDER:
Holaxonia
FAMILY:
Plexauridae

SIZE: Colony height
$^1/_2$ - 7 ft.
DEPTH: 3 - 250 ft.

Porous Sea Rods
Note pore-like polyp apertures.

Tall colony.
[far left]

Branch detail.
[left]

Porous Sea Rods
Bush-like colony.

Gorgonians

VISUAL ID: Sea rod colonies of this genus can be recognized when their polyps are retracted, leaving prominently extended calyces (with one exception, *E. knighti,* whose polyp apertures resemble those of Porous Sea Rods). Most branch laterally in a flat plane that resembles a candelabrum. Only a few of the over one dozen species can be distinguished underwater. All remaining species of this genus are so individually variable in appearance, and yet similar to one another, that they cannot easily be distinguished visually. Microscopic examination is required for positive identification. Colors vary greatly from light brown through yellow-brown, brown, reddish purple, purple and gray.

ABUNDANCE & DISTRIBUTION: Common South Florida, Bahamas, Caribbean.

HABITAT & BEHAVIOR: Inhabit most reef environments and adjacent sandy substrates.

Knobby Sea Rods
Polyp detail.

VISUAL ID: The close-set, swollen, tubular calyces of these candelabrum-shaped colonies easily distinguish them from other members of the genus. Colonies compact with stout branches. Light yellowish brown.

ABUNDANCE & DISTRIBUTION: Common Northwest Caribbean; uncommon to occasional South Florida, Bahamas, eastern and southern Caribbean.

HABITAT & BEHAVIOR: Inhabit most reef environments, from shallow, turbulent hard bottoms to patch reefs, deeper outer reefs and along wall lips.

SIMILAR SPECIES: Tube-knob Candelabrum, *E. laxispica,* distinguished by longer, more widely spaced, tube-like calyces. Uncommon to rare.

KNOBBY SEA RODS
Eunicea spp.
SUBORDER:
Holaxonia
FAMILY:
Plexauridae

SIZE: Colony height
$^1/_2$ - 3 ft.
DEPTH: 3 - 100 ft.

Knobby Sea Rods
Knobby calyx detail.

SWOLLEN-KNOB CANDELABRUM
Eunicea mammosa
SUBORDER:
Holaxonia
FAMILY:
Plexauridae

SIZE: Colony height
$^3/_4$ - 1 ft.
DEPTH: 5 - 90 ft.

continued next page

Swollen-knob Candelabrum

Calyx detail; note close-set, swollen tubular form.

VISUAL ID: The diagonally upward projecting calyces distinguish this species from other members of the genus. In side view the calyces appear as tiny shelves with diagonal supports. Calyces' lower lips slightly upturned. Colonies grow in two forms: form *succinea* are low, wide, candelabrum-shaped with thick end branches; form *plantaginea* are tall and bushy with thin end branches, calyces' lower lips more upturned. (Similar Warty Sea Rod [next] distinguished by thicker branches and gaping calyces.) Light yellowish brown to brown.

ABUNDANCE & DISTRIBUTION: Common South Florida, Bahamas, Caribbean.

HABITAT & BEHAVIOR: Inhabit shallow, turbulent hard bottoms and patch reefs.

Shelf-knob Sea Rod

Calyx detail; note shelf-like appearance.

Swollen-knob Candelabrum

continued from previous page

Colony with polyps retracted.

SHELF-KNOB SEA ROD

Eunicea succinea

SUBORDER:
Holaxonia
FAMILY:
Plexauridae

form *succinea.*

SIZE: Colony height
$^{3}/_{4}$ - 2 ft.
DEPTH: 5 - 50 ft.

Shelf-knob Sea Rod
form *plantaginea.*

Gorgonians

VISUAL ID: Only Knobby Sea Rod colony with thick, cylindrical, non-tapering branches that is tall, bushy, and does not branch in a single plane. (Can be confused with Shelf-knob Sea Rod, form *plantaginea* [previous], distinguished by their thinner end branches and shelf-like calyces.) Dichotomous branching. Extended polyps give colony yellowish brown appearance. Calyces low and gaping.

ABUNDANCE & DISTRIBUTION: Common South Florida, Bahamas, Caribbean.

HABITAT & BEHAVIOR: Inhabit most reef environments; most common on inshore reefs.

Warty Sea Rod
Polyp detail.

VISUAL ID: When fully contracted the low, circular, somewhat swollen calyces with round, central apertures distinguish this species from other members of the genus. Often form low, bushy, shrub-like colonies, occasionally tall with widely spaced branches. Rods light to dark gray; polyps yellow-brown to brown.

ABUNDANCE & DISTRIBUTION: Common to occasional South Florida, Bahamas, Caribbean.

HABITAT & BEHAVIOR: Inhabit shallow, turbulent hard bottoms and patch reefs.

WARTY SEA ROD
Eunicea calyculata
SUBORDER:
Holaxonia
FAMILY:
Plexauridae

SIZE: Colony height
1 - 3 ft.
DEPTH: 10 - 110 ft.

Warty Sea Rod
Calyx detail.

DOUGHNUT SEA ROD
Eunicea fusca
SUBORDER:
Holaxonia
FAMILY:
Plexauridae

SIZE: Colony height
$^1/_2$ - $1^1/_2$ ft.
DEPTH: 10 - 75 ft.

continued next page

Gorgonians

VISUAL ID: Sea rod colonies of this genus can be recognized when their polyps are retracted, leaving elliptical or slit-like apertures that may or may not have slightly raised rims (calyces). With one exception, Giant Slit-pore Sea Rod [next], all of the six species of this genus are so individually variable in appearance, and yet similar to one another, that they cannot easily be distinguished visually. Microscopic examination is required for positive identification. Colonies are generally bushy with stout stalks, and branch dichotomously. Colors vary greatly from light brown to yellow-brown, brown, reddish purple, purple and gray.

ABUNDANCE & DISTRIBUTION: Common South Florida, Bahamas, Caribbean.

HABITAT & BEHAVIOR: Inhabit most clear water reef environments.

Slit-pore Sea Rods

Colony with polyps retracted.

Doughnut Sea Rod

continued from previous page

Comparison of Doughnut Sea Rod, (left) and Bent Sea Rod (right).

Polyp Detail
[far left]

Calyx Detail
[left]

SLIT-PORE SEA RODS
Plexaurella spp.
SUBORDER:
Holaxonia
FAMILY:
Plexauridae

SIZE: Colony height
$^1/_2$ - $3^1/_2$ ft.
DEPTH: 3 - 160 ft.

Slit-pore Sea Rods

Retracted polyp detail; note slit-like aperture.

VISUAL ID: Colonies very tall with thick stalks and sparse, dichotomous branching. Branch tips usually somewhat enlarged. Slit-like apertures of retracted polyps are on slightly raised, well-separated mounds. Pale gray to tan or light brown.

ABUNDANCE & DISTRIBUTION: Common to occasional South Florida, Bahamas, Caribbean.

HABITAT & BEHAVIOR: Primarily inhabit clear water patch and fore reefs.

NOTE: Also commonly known as "Nodding Plexaurella."

Giant Slit-pore Sea Rod
Retracted polyp detail; note slightly raised lips and slit-like pores.

VISUAL ID: Low, broad fan-shaped colonies, branched laterally with only occasional dichotomous secondary branching, all in single planes. Branches tend to be tightly compacted. Hard, rough calyces with sharply spiked tips extend prominently. Pale yellowish brown to light brown; polyps white.

ABUNDANCE & DISTRIBUTION: Common to occasional South Florida, Bahamas, Caribbean.

HABITAT & BEHAVIOR: Inhabit wide range of shallow to moderate environments.

NOTE: Photographed specimen was collected and visual identification confirmed by examination of wood-like central branch axis which is conspicuously flattened in this species.

SIMILAR SPECIES: Open Spiny Sea Fan, *M. atlantica*, visually distinguished by their tendency to be taller and having more open branching. Uncommon. Positive identification requires specimen examination of the wood-like central branch axis which is not conspicuously flattened.

GIANT SLIT-PORE SEA ROD
Plexaurella nutans
SUBORDER:
Holaxonia
FAMILY:
Plexauridae

SIZE: Colony height
2 - 4 1/2 ft.
DEPTH: 30 - 160 ft.

SPINY SEA FAN
Muricea muricata
SUBORDER:
Holaxonia
FAMILY:
Plexauridae

SIZE: Colony height
4 - 12 in.
DEPTH: 0 - 60 ft.

continued next page

Gorgonians

VISUAL ID: Colonies have open pinnate branching in single planes; older colonies may be somewhat bushy. Branchlets short, stiff and widely spaced. Hard, rough calyces; each has a distinctive, long, sharp terminal spine. Branches whitish to light gray or yellow-brown; polyps yellowish brown.

ABUNDANCE & DISTRIBUTION: Occasional Caribbean.

HABITAT & BEHAVIOR: Inhabit clear water, moderate to deep fore reef environments.

SIMILAR SPECIES: Pinnate Spiney Sea Fan, *M. pendula,* because of its distinctive red color is described on page 77.

Long Spine Sea Fan
Branch/polyp detail; note open pinnate branching.

Spiny Sea Fan
*continued from
previous page*

Unusually tall colony.

*Polyp detail.
[far left]*

*Calyx detail.
[left]*

LONG SPINE SEA FAN
Muricea pinnata
SUBORDER:
Holaxonia
FAMILY:
Plexauridae

SIZE: Colony height
8 - 18 in.
DEPTH: 40 - 120 ft.

Long Spine Sea Fan
*Branch/calyx detail;
note long, terminal spines.*

Gorgonians

VISUAL ID: Tall, bushy colonies, not branched in single planes. Branched laterally near base, but toward top tend to branch pinnately. Hard, rough, close-set calyces extend prominently with sharply spiked lower lips. Branches yellow to yellowish brown, orange or amber; polyps white. (Similar Delicate Spiny Sea Rod [next] can usually be distinguished by their bluish white to gray branches, thinner branches, more projecting calyx lips and deeper habitat.)

ABUNDANCE & DISTRIBUTION: Common to occasional Florida's west coast and from West Palm through the Keys, Bahamas, Caribbean.

HABITAT & BEHAVIOR: Inhabit wide range of shallow to moderate environments, from sandy bottoms to sloping rocky substrates and patch reefs.

NOTE: Small sample of pictured specimen was collected and visual identification confirmed by microscopic examination of spicules.

Orange Spiny Sea Rod
Polyp detail.

VISUAL ID: Tall, bushy colonies, laterally branched, but not in single planes. Branches slender, flexible and long. Narrow, hard, rough calyces extend prominently upward with sharply spiked lower lips. Branches bluish gray to bluish white, occasionally yellowish; polyps white. (Compare similar Orange Spiny Sea Rod [previous].)

ABUNDANCE & DISTRIBUTION: Common to occasional Florida's west coast and from West Palm through the Keys, Bahamas, Caribbean.

HABITAT & BEHAVIOR: Inhabit wide range of moderate to deep environments, from sloping rocky substrates to patch reefs.

NOTE: Small sample of pictured specimen was collected and visual identification confirmed by microscopic examination of spicules.

ORANGE SPINY SEA ROD

Muricea elongata

SUBORDER:
Holaxonia
FAMILY:
Plexauridae

SIZE: Colony height
1 - 1 $^1/_2$ ft.
DEPTH: 10 - 70 ft.

Orange Spiny Sea Rod

Branch/calyx detail; note orangish color.

DELICATE SPINY SEA ROD

Muricea laxa

SUBORDER:
Holaxonia
FAMILY:
Plexauridae

SIZE: Colony height
8 - 12 in.
DEPTH: 60 - 420 ft.

continued next page **47**

Gorgonians

**Delicate Spiny
Sea Rod**
Branch/polyp detail.

VISUAL ID: Colonies form bushy clusters of tall, plume-like branches. Numerous short, slender, round branchlets extend from all sides of main branches. Small, closely set polyp apertures are scattered randomly on all sides of main and secondary branches. (Similar Sea Feather Plumes [next] have polyps in rows, series or bands.) Apertures have small, lower shelf-like lips, giving the surface a somewhat rough texture. Most commonly purple, occasionally gray, and may be tinged with yellow.

ABUNDANCE & DISTRIBUTION: Common South Florida, Bahamas, Caribbean.

HABITAT & BEHAVIOR: Inhabit most clear water patch reef environments.

ADDITIONAL SPECIES: Sulphur Sea Plume, *M. sulphurea*, yellow, low, bushy, shrub-like colonies; secondary branches on all sides of main branches and polyps randomly scattered on all sides; Puerto Rico through Lesser Antilles. Deep Water Sea Plume, *M. petila*, tall, main branches with widely spaced, pinnately branching secondary branches; violet to lavender; below 100 feet; South Florida, Bahamas.

Rough Sea Plume
*Branch detail;
note branchlets
extend in
all directions.*

Delicate Spiny Sea Rod
continued from previous page

Branch/calyx detail; note bluish gray color.

ROUGH SEA PLUME
Muriceopsis flavida
SUBORDER:
Holaxonia
FAMILY:
Plexauridae

SIZE: Colony height 8 - 30 in.
DEPTH: 3 - 110 ft.

Rough Sea Plume
Gray variety.

Gorgonians

VISUAL ID: Bushy clusters of tall, feather-like plumes typify this genus. Pinnately branching secondary branches or branchlets, lying more or less in single planes, extend from the main branches. Polyps in rows, series or bands, rather than random distribution on all sides of branch. Calyces absent or indistinct. Most commonly purple to gray branches, occasionally bright to pale yellow or yellow-brown. Polyps generally cream to brownish or grayish. With two exceptions, Slimy Sea Plume [next] and Bipinnate Sea Plume, *Pseudopterogordia bipinnata*, [next page], all of the remaining dozen or so species of this genus are so individually variable in appearance, and yet similar to one another, that they cannot easily be distinguished visually. Microscopic examination is required for positive identification.

ABUNDANCE & DISTRIBUTION: Common South Florida, Bahamas, Caribbean.

HABITAT & BEHAVIOR: Inhabit most reef environments, from shallow, seaward sandy areas to patch reefs to deep clear water reefs along drop-offs.

Sea Plumes
Several species can exceed seven feet in height.

VISUAL ID: Colonies form bushy clusters of tall, feather-like plumes. Long branchlets extend pinnately from primary branches. Primary branches most commonly purple to violet, occasionally pale yellow. Living colonies produce large amounts of mucus, causing the branches to feel slimy, distinguishing them from similar appearing species. (To avoid injury to a colony it should only be lightly touched near the base, which will feel soft, slick and slimy.)

ABUNDANCE & DISTRIBUTION: Common South Florida, Bahamas, Caribbean.

HABITAT & BEHAVIOR: Inhabit most reef environments, from shallow hard bottoms to patch reefs to deep clear water reefs along drop-offs.

SEA PLUMES
Pseudopterogorgia spp.
SUBORDER:
Holaxonia
FAMILY:
Gorgoniidae

SIZE: Colony height
1 - 7 ft.
DEPTH: 3 - 180 ft.

Sea Plumes
*Large colony
with polyps
retracted.*

SLIMY SEA PLUME
*Pseudopterogorgia
americana*
SUBORDER:
Holaxonia
FAMILY:
Gorgoniidae

SIZE: Colony height
2¹/₂ - 3¹/₂ ft.
DEPTH: 5 - 150 ft.

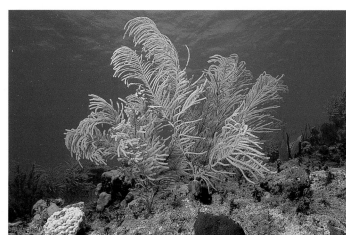

Gorgonians

VISUAL ID: Colonies generally grow in single planes with broadly spread primary and secondary branches. Paired branchlets extend from branches at regularly spaced intervals. These branchlets, distinctive of this species, are short, blunt, stiff and extend directly opposite one another at almost right angles. Branches most commonly purple to violet, occasionally bright yellow to whitish.

ABUNDANCE & DISTRIBUTION: Common South Florida, Bahamas, Caribbean.

HABITAT & BEHAVIOR: Inhabit moderate to deep, clear water patch reefs.

VISUAL ID: Small, bushy and highly branched colonies. Branches quite flat and narrow with polyps extending from swollen, slit-like apertures along the thin edges. (Similar Grooved-blade Sea Whip [next] is distinguished by polyps extending from common groove along thin edges.) Branches bright yellow to green to olive with purple edges, occasionally all purple; polyps white to cream.

ABUNDANCE & DISTRIBUTION: Common South Florida, Bahamas, Caribbean. Can be abundant in localized areas.

HABITAT & BEHAVIOR: Inhabit a wide range of shallower, inshore environments, from back reef areas to patch reefs.

BIPINNATE SEA PLUME
Pseudopterogorgia bipinnata
SUBORDER:
Holaxonia
FAMILY:
Gorgoniidae

SIZE: Colony height
1 - 2 ft.
DEPTH: 45 - 180 ft.

Bipinnate Sea Plume
Colony with polyps retracted.

Branch detail with polyps extended.
[far left]

Branch detail with polyps retracted.
[left]

YELLOW SEA WHIP
Pterogorgia citrina
SUBORDER:
Holaxonia
FAMILY:
Gorgoniidae

SIZE: Colony height
4 - 12 in.
Branch width $1/4$ in.
DEPTH: 3 - 40 ft.

continued next page 53

Gorgonians

VISUAL ID: Colonies heavily branched, more or less in single planes. Long, flexible branches quite flat and wide, tapering somewhat from base to end. Polyps extend from a groove that runs along the thin edges. (Similar Yellow Sea Whip [previous] is distinguished by polyps extending from slit-like apertures along thin edges.) Branches olive to gray, occasionally light purple; polyps white to cream.

ABUNDANCE & DISTRIBUTION: Occasional South Florida, Bahamas, Caribbean.

HABITAT & BEHAVIOR: Inhabit a wide range of inshore environments, from back reef areas of sand and rubble to patch reefs of moderate depth.

Grooved-blade Sea Whip
Polyp/groove detail.

Yellow Sea Whip
continued from previous page
Color variation.

Calyx/polyp detail; note polyps do not extend from a slit-like groove.
[far left]

Color varieties.
[left]

GROOVED-BLADE SEA WHIP
Pterogorgia guadalupensis
SUBORDER:
Holaxonia
FAMILY:
Gorgoniidae

SIZE: Colony height
$^1/_2$ - 2 ft.
Branch width $^1/_4$ - $^1/_2$ in.
DEPTH: 3 - 60 ft.

Grooved-blade Sea Whip
Purplish variation.

Gorgonians

VISUAL ID: Colonies large, bushy and highly branched. A cross-section of a branch is "Y" or "X" shaped. Branches taper from bases toward the terminal ends and often twist. Ends may occasionally be a flattened blade-shape. Polyps extend from a groove that runs along the branches' thin edges. Olive to brown to gray, occasionally purple or with purplish tints. Edge of grooves usually purple; polyps white to cream.

ABUNDANCE & DISTRIBUTION: Common to occasional South Florida, Bahamas, Caribbean. Can be abundant in localized areas.

HABITAT & BEHAVIOR: Inhabit a wide range of inshore environments, from back reef areas of sand and rubble to patch reefs of moderate depth.

Angular Sea Whip
Polyp/groove detail.

VISUAL ID: Colonies form large fans that grow in single planes. Fans are composed of tightly-meshed, interconnected network of branches that are round or slightly flattened on the outer surface. (Compare similar Venus Sea Fan [next].) In Florida always purple, remainder of range commonly purple, occasionally yellow or brownish.

ABUNDANCE & DISTRIBUTION: Common South Florida, Bahamas, Caribbean.

HABITAT & BEHAVIOR: Prefer clear water with some movement. Inhabit the seaward side of shallow reefs, slopes and patch reefs. Only occasionally on reefs and along the lips of drop-offs deeper than 50 feet.

ANGULAR SEA WHIP
Pterogorgia anceps
SUBORDER:
Holaxonia
FAMILY:
Gorgoniidae

SIZE: Colony height
1 - 2 ft.
Branch width ⅛ - ¼ in.
DEPTH: 12 - 65 ft.

Angular Sea Whip
*Colony with polyps
retracted.*

COMMON SEA FAN
Gorgonia ventalina
SUBORDER:
Holaxonia
FAMILY:
Gorgoniidae

SIZE: Colony height
2 - 6 ft.
DEPTH: 3 - 100 ft.

continued next page

Gorgonians

Common Sea Fan
*Branch detail;
outer surface flattened.*

VISUAL ID: Colonies form large fans that grow in single planes. Fans are composed of tightly-meshed, interconnected network of branches. Branches' inner edges are distinctly flattened at right angles to the fans' surfaces. (Compare similar Common Sea Fan [previous].) Occasionally have small branchlets growing from their flat sides. Commonly yellow, occasionally lavender to gray.

ABUNDANCE & DISTRIBUTION: Abundant Bahamas; common to uncommon Caribbean; rare South Florida.

HABITAT & BEHAVIOR: Prefer clear water with some movement. Commonly inhabit the seaward side of shallow reef slopes and patch reefs. Only occasionally on reefs and along lips of drop-offs deeper than 35 feet. In Caribbean often inhabit shallow back reef areas.

NOTE: Also commonly known as "Bahamian Sea Fan."

Venus Sea Fan
*Branching detail;
note flattening
at right angle
to fan's surface.*

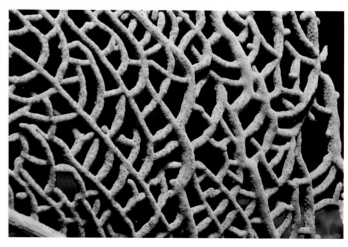

Common Sea Fan

continued from previous page

VENUS SEA FAN

Gorgonia flabellum

SUBORDER:
Holaxonia
FAMILY:
Gorgoniidae

SIZE: Colony height
2 - 3¹/₂ ft.
DEPTH: 3 - 100 ft.

Venus Sea Fan

Purple variation.

Gorgonians

VISUAL ID: Colonies form small fans that grow in single planes. Fans are composed of a widely-meshed pattern of branches. Secondary branches extending from ascending primary branches are generally pinnate and do not always unite or interconnect. In deep water white to pale violet or yellow; in shallow water tend to be yellow, occasionally with purplish tints.

ABUNDANCE & DISTRIBUTION: Occasional Caribbean. Not known from Florida or Bahamas.

HABITAT & BEHAVIOR: Prefer clear water with some movement. Inhabit wide range of reef environments, but most abundant below 50 feet where Common and Venus Sea Fans [previous] are not as numerous.

Wide-mesh Sea Fan
Branch structure detail; note sparse interconnecting of branches.

VISUAL ID: Branch dichotomously in single planes to form huge fan-shaped colonies. Outer surfaces of branches flattened with polyps extending in two parallel rows from narrow inner edges. Red-brown to orange-brown, dark brown and gray.

ABUNDANCE & DISTRIBUTION: Abundant to occasional East Florida, Bahamas, Caribbean.

HABITAT & BEHAVIOR: Inhabit most deep water environments, from patch reefs to deep slopes, canyons, crevices and along walls. Prefer clear water areas with some current. Most common below 60 feet. Polyps often extended, especially when there is water movement.

WIDE-MESH SEA FAN
Gorgonia mariae
SUBORDER:
Holaxonia
FAMILY:
Gorgoniidae

SIZE: Colony height
6 - 12 in.
DEPTH: 3 - 156 ft.

Wide-mesh Sea Fan
Yellow variation.

DEEPWATER SEA FAN
Iciligorgia schrammi
SUBORDER:
Scleraxonia
FAMILY:
Anthothelidae

SIZE: Colony height
1 - 4 ft.
DEPTH: 35 - 1200 ft.

continued next page 61

Gorgonians

Deepwater Sea Fan
Polyp detail.

VISUAL ID: Form both slender branching and stout, rod-like colonies. Cone-shaped calyces protrude noticeably. Red stems with red calyces or red stems with yellow calyx rims or yellow to orange stems with reddish, violet or purple calyx rims; polyps white and somewhat translucent. (Stout, rod-like colonies similar to Brilliant Sea Fingers [next] distinguished by smooth rod surfaces.)

ABUNDANCE & DISTRIBUTION: Common to occasional South Florida, Bahamas, Caribbean.

HABITAT & BEHAVIOR: Inhabit wide range of moderate to deep environments, from patch reefs to sandy and rocky substrates to shaded areas under ledge overhangs along deep walls.

NOTE: A small sample of photographed specimen was collected and visual identification confirmed by microscopic examination of spicules.

Colorful Sea Rod
Branch/polyp detail.

Deepwater Sea Fan
continued from previous page

Colony with polyps extended.

COLORFUL SEA ROD
Diodogorgia nodulifera
SUBORDER:
Scleraxonia
FAMILY:
Anthothelidae

SIZE: Colony Height
4 - 12 in.
DEPTH: 45 - 600 ft.

Colorful Sea Rod
Orange stem, reddish calyx variation.

Gorgonians

VISUAL ID: Colonies usually form short, stout, smooth cylindrical rods; occasionally tall, with several branches. Bright red to pinkish red, orange and yellowish orange; polyps translucent white.

ABUNDANCE & DISTRIBUTION: Occasional East Florida. Not reported Bahamas or Caribbean.

HABITAT & BEHAVIOR: Inhabit current-swept areas with hard, rocky substrates. Tend to be red off North Florida and orange off South Florida.

Brilliant Sea Fingers
Polyp detail.

VISUAL ID: Scraggly, bushy, occasionally fan-shaped colonies with relatively thin branches and long protruding calyces. Only gorgonian in South Florida, Bahamas and Caribbean (within safe diving limits) with both orange to red stems and polyps.

ABUNDANCE & DISTRIBUTION: Common Florida; occasional to uncommon Bahamas, Caribbean.

HABITAT & BEHAVIOR: In Florida inhabit moderate to deep patch reefs and rocky/sandy substrates; colonies often quite bushy (opposite). In Caribbean, tend to inhabit only deep water environments over 100 feet, especially under ledge overhangs and cave ceilings; colonies often in fan-like growth pattern (next page, right).

BRILLIANT SEA FINGERS
Titanideum frauenfeldii
SUBORDER:
Scleraxonia
FAMILY:
Anthothelidae

SIZE: Colony height
3 in. - 2 ft.
DEPTH: 50 - 780 ft.

Brilliant Sea Fingers
Typical rod-like colonies.

RED POLYP OCTOCORAL
Swiftia exserta
SUBORDER:
Holaxonia
FAMILY:
Plexauridae

SIZE: Colony height
6 - 18 in.
DEPTH: 40 - 260 ft.

continued next page

Gorgonians

Red Polyp Octocoral
Polyp detail.

VISUAL ID: Colonies form single, long, whip-like stalks that taper slightly from base to tip. Bright orange to orange-red to red; polyps white.

ABUNDANCE & DISTRIBUTION: Common to occasional East Florida, Bahamas, Caribbean.

HABITAT & BEHAVIOR: Inhabit deep, clear water environments, especially on steep slopes and walls. Attach to rocky substrate.

Devil's Sea Whip
Polyp detail.

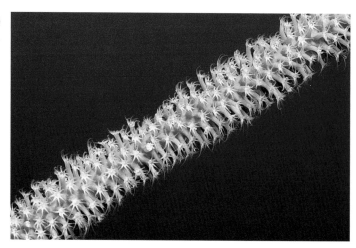

Red Polyp Octocoral
*continued from
previous page*

Fan-like growth pattern.

DEVIL'S SEA WHIP
Ellisella barbadensis
SUBORDER:
Holaxonia
FAMILY:
Ellisellidae

SIZE: Colony height
2 - 8 ft.
Base diameter
$^{1}/_{4}$ - $^{1}/_{2}$ in.
DEPTH: 65 - 1600 ft.

Gorgonians

VISUAL ID: Tall, erect colonies branch dichotomously from short base stalks. Branches long, stiff, and whip-like. (Similar Bushy Sea Whips [next page] occasionally grow upright, but are easily distinguished by their short branches that tend to rebranch several times.) Branches number from a few to over two dozen. Bright orange to orange-red to red; polyps white.

ABUNDANCE & DISTRIBUTION: Occasional Florida, Bahamas, Caribbean.

HABITAT & BEHAVIOR: Attach to rocky substrates in deep, clear water environments, especially on steep slopes and walls. In Caribbean most common below 100 feet, but along Florida Gulf Coast as shallow as 50 feet.

SIMILAR SPECIES: *E. grandis* may be indistinguishable underwater. However, the genus *Ellisella* needs revision before scientific accuracy in identifying and distinguishing species is possible.

Long Sea Whip
Polyp detail.

VISUAL ID: Fan-shaped colonies, formed by some lateral branching off main stalks and profuse dichotomous rebranching, all in single planes. Bright orange to orange to red; polyps white.

ABUNDANCE & DISTRIBUTION: Occasional South Florida, Bahamas, Caribbean.

HABITAT & BEHAVIOR: Inhabit deep, clear water environments, especially under ledge overhangs, on cave ceilings, and along canyons, crevices and walls. Rare within safe diving limits.

LONG SEA WHIP
Ellisella elongata
SUBORDER:
Holaxonia
FAMILY:
Ellisellidae

SIZE: Colony height
3 - 5 ft.
Base diameter
$^{1}/_{4}$ - $^{1}/_{2}$ in.
DEPTH: 50 - 720 ft.

ORANGE DEEP
WATER FAN
Nicella goreaui
SUBORDER:
Holaxonia
FAMILY:
Ellisellidae

SIZE: Colony height
$^{1}/_{2}$ - 1 $^{1}/_{2}$ ft.
DEPTH: 100 - 260 ft.

continued next page

Gorgonians

Orange Deep Water Fan
Polyp detail.

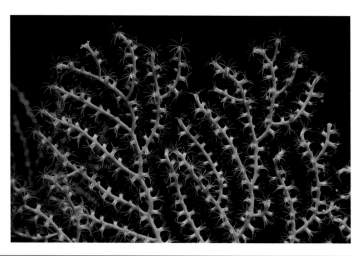

VISUAL ID: Numerous short, stiff, whip-like branches and secondary branches extend from base stalks. (Similar Long Sea Whip [previous page] distinguished by branches that are long and generally without secondary branches.) Branching and rebranching are both lateral and dichotomous. Bright orange to orange to red; polyps white.

ABUNDANCE & DISTRIBUTION: Common to occasional South Florida, Bahamas, Caribbean.

HABITAT & BEHAVIOR: Inhabit deep, clear water environments, especially under ledge overhangs, on cave ceilings, and along canyons, crevices and walls. Rarely grow upright like similar Long Sea Whip [previous page].

Orange Deep Water Fan

continued from previous page

Polyps retracted.

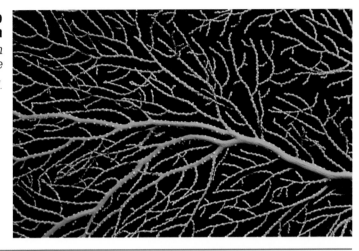

BUSHY SEA WHIP
Nicella schmitti
SUBORDER:
Holaxonia
FAMILY:
Ellisellidae

Polyp detail.
[far left]
Bushy branch detail.
[left]

SIZE: Colony height
1 - 2 ft.
Base diameter
$^{1}/_{4}$ - $^{1}/_{2}$ in.
DEPTH: 65 - 220 ft.

71

Gorgonians

VISUAL ID: Colonies form long, straight, stiff, moderately branched, whip-like stalks. Polyps in multiple rows along two sides. Calyces do not protrude when polyps are retracted. Stalks' color highly variable, including shades of lavender, violet, purple, red, orange and yellow; polyps translucent white.

ABUNDANCE & DISTRIBUTION: Common both coasts of Florida.

HABITAT & BEHAVIOR: Inhabit most environments, especially in areas with hard substrate and some sand.

NOTE: Small sample of pictured specimen was collected and visual identification confirmed by microscopic examination of spicules. Formerly classified *Lophogorgia,* which is no longer considered a separate genus.

Colorful Sea Whip
Orange variation.

Colorful Sea Whip
Branch/polyp detail.

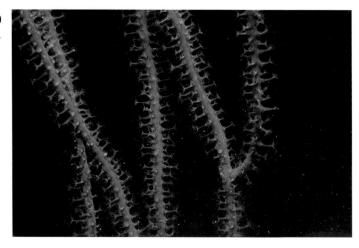

COLORFUL SEA WHIP
Leptogorgia virgulata
SUBORDER:
Holaxonia
FAMILY:
Gorgoniidae

SIZE: Colony height
$1/2$ - $1 1/2$ ft.
DEPTH: 25 - 130 ft.

Colorful Sea Whip
Violet variation.

73

Gorgonians

VISUAL ID: Colonies thickly branched, generally in single planes. Branches somewhat flattened. Polyps alternate in rows along edges. Rows are separated by distinct grooves on older main branches. Calyces generally more prominent in older parts of colony. Branches orange to red, reddish purple and purple; polyps translucent to white.

ABUNDANCE & DISTRIBUTION: Common both coasts of Florida. Not known from Bahamas, Caribbean.

HABITAT & BEHAVIOR: Inhabit most environments, especially in areas with hard substrate and some sand.

NOTE: Small sample of pictured specimen was collected and visual identification confirmed by microscopic examination of spicules. Formerly classified *Lophogorgia,* which is no longer considered a separate genus.

Regal Sea Fan
Branch detail with polyps extended.

VISUAL ID: Small, openly pinnate branching colonies. Commonly branch in a single plane, but may be somewhat bushy. Low, blunt calyces in single rows along the two edges of outer branches; thicker branches have double rows. Branches orange-red to red to reddish purple; polyps translucent white.

ABUNDANCE & DISTRIBUTION: Occasional Florida, southeastern and southern Caribbean. Not reported Bahamas or remainder of Caribbean.

HABITAT & BEHAVIOR: Inhabit most environments, especially in areas with hard substrate and some sand.

NOTE: Small sample of pictured specimen was collected and visual identification confirmed by microscopic examination of spicules. Formerly classified *Lophogorgia,* which is no longer considered a separate genus.

REGAL SEA FAN
Leptogorgia hebes
SUBORDER:
Holaxonia
FAMILY:
Gorgoniidae

SIZE: Colony Height
$\frac{1}{2}$ - 1$\frac{1}{2}$ ft.
DEPTH: 25 - 130 ft.

Regal Sea Fan
Branch detail with polyps retracted.

CARMINE SEA SPRAY
Leptogorgia miniata
SUBORDER:
Holaxonia
FAMILY:
Gorgoniidae

SIZE: Colony Height
2 - 5 in.
DEPTH: 40 - 120 ft.

continued next page 75

Gorgonians

Carmine Sea Spray

Branch detail with polyps extended.

VISUAL ID: Fan-shaped colonies with regular pinnate branching in a single plane. Branches stiff, widely spaced and somewhat enlarged at the tips. Hard, rough, prickly calyces, without terminal spikes are openly spaced and protrude noticeably. Branches brownish yellow to brownish orange to orange or red; polyps' tentacles translucent to white, centers yellowish to orange or red.

ABUNDANCE & DISTRIBUTION: Occasional both Florida coasts. Not reported Bahamas, Caribbean.

HABITAT & BEHAVIOR: Inhabit clear water, moderate to deep fore reef environments.

SIMILAR SPECIES: Five additional species of *Muricea* are described on pages 43-47.

NOTE: Small sample of pictured specimen was collected and visual identification confirmed by microscopic examination of spicules.

Pinnate Spiny Sea Fan

Polyp detail.

Carmine Sea Spray

continued from previous page

Bushy colony.

PINNATE SPINY SEA FAN

Muricea pendula

SUBORDER:
Holaxonia
FAMILY:
Plexauridae

SIZE: Colony height
8 - 18 in.
DEPTH: 40 - 120 ft.

Pinnate Spiny Sea Fan

Branch detail.

Gorgonians

VISUAL ID: Lateral branching colonies generally in a single plane; larger colonies tend to be somewhat bushy. Branches of living specimens are yellow-brown to reddish brown to grayish red. Normally extended polyps bright red to pink, often with white centers.

ABUNDANCE & DISTRIBUTION: Common off North Florida Atlantic coast. Additional distribution within safe diving limits not reported. Deep dwelling specimens reported from Dry Tortugas and eastern Caribbean.

HABITAT & BEHAVIOR: Inhabit areas of hard substrate.

NOTE: Samples of pictured specimens were collected and identification made by microscopic examination of spicules.

White Eye Sea Spray
Colonies with partially retracted and retracted polyps.

WHITE EYE SEA SPRAY
Thesea nivea
SUBORDER:
Holaxonia
FAMILY:
Gorgoniidae

SIZE: Colony 6 - 18 in.
DEPTH: 75-1,200 ft.

White Eye Sea Spray
Bushy colony.

White Eye Sea Spray
Polyp detail;
note branch color.

Polyp detail;
without white centers.
[far left]

Polyp detail;
with white centers.
[left]

79

Gorgonians

VISUAL ID: Colonies thickly branched, generally in single planes, often fan-shaped. Polyps usually extended and protrude dramatically from relatively thin stems. Polyps bright yellow to yellow-gold; stems yellowish to tan or brown.

ABUNDANCE & DISTRIBUTION: Common Northwest Caribbean. Not reported remainder of Caribbean, Florida or Bahamas.

HABITAT & BEHAVIOR: Inhabit deep reefs, especially along drop-offs and walls. Most common in protected areas, under ledge overhangs, wall undercuts, narrow canyons and crevices; occasionally exposed on reef tops.

NOTE: Small sample of pictured specimen was collected and microscopic examination confirmed this as a previously uncollected, undescribed species. Species first described in 1990 from locations off Brazil, between 22-100 feet. Previously unknown in Caribbean.

VISUAL ID: Colonies form rigid stalks with large, prominent, white to translucent polyps. Stalks tipped with single polyp; below, secondary (daughter) polyps grow at intervals of about ³/₈ inch. Bright red to pink. Polyps usually extended. Stalks often encrusted and/or overgrown with algae, sponge and other organisms.

ABUNDANCE & DISTRIBUTION: Uncommon Bahamas, eastern Caribbean. Not reported Florida, West or Northwest Caribbean.

HABITAT & BEHAVIOR: Inhabit deep shaded areas, such as narrow canyon walls and caves. Prefer areas regularly swept with current.

NOTE: Photographed specimen was collected (USNM 1015356) and visual identification confirmed by examination with scanning electron microscope. This species' closest relative is *S. rubra* from the Indian Ocean. Previously classified in the genus *Telesto*.

GOLDEN SEA SPRAY
Heterogorgia uatumani
SUBORDER:
Holaxonia
FAMILY:
Plexauridae

SIZE: Colony Height
$^1/_2$ - 1 ft.
DEPTH: 75 - 150 ft.

Golden Sea Spray
Small colony.

Polyp detail.
[far left]

Fan-shaped colony.
[left]

RIGID RED TELESTO
Stereotelesto corallina
FAMILY:
Clavulariidae
SUBFAMILY:
Telestinae

SIZE: Colony Height
$^3/_4$ - 2 in.
DEPTH: 75 - 600 ft.

VISUAL ID: Colonies form dense clusters of tangled, branched stems with large, prominent, white polyps. Stems tipped with single polyps; below, secondary (daughter) polyps grow in pairs or groups of three at about the same level. White to pale pink stalks have eight longitudinal grooves. Polyps usually extended. Stems often encrusted and/or overgrown with algae, sponge and other organisms.

ABUNDANCE & DISTRIBUTION: Occasional South Florida, Bahamas, Caribbean.

HABITAT & BEHAVIOR: Considered a fouling organism. Can be abundant in shallow, rocky areas and under docks. In deeper water common on shipwrecks — often the first octocorallian to inhabit new wrecks/artificial reefs. Uncommon on reefs and walls.

NOTE: Previously classified in the genus *Telesto.*

VISUAL ID: Colonies form clusters of branched stems with large, prominent, white polyps. Stems tipped with single polyp; below, secondary (daughter) polyps extend from all sides. Yellow to orange to pale red stalks have eight longitudinal grooves. Polyps usually extended. Stems often encrusted and/or overgrown with algae, sponge and other organisms.

ABUNDANCE & DISTRIBUTION: Occasional Florida's Atlantic coast from West Palm Beach northward to Carolinas. Not reported Bahamas, Caribbean.

HABITAT & BEHAVIOR: Inhabit areas of rocky outcroppings and hard rubble, also attach to wrecks.

SIMILAR SPECIES: Red Telesto, *T. sanguinea,* is bright coral red, 75-350 feet, both Florida coasts and Keys.

NOTE: Photographed specimen was collected and visual identification confirmed by microscopic examination.

WHITE TELESTO
Carijoa riisei
FAMILY:
Clavulariidae
SUBFAMILY:
Telestinae

White Telesto

Colony encrusting shipwreck.
[far left]

Polyp detail.
[left]

SIZE: Colony Height
2 - 10 in.
DEPTH: 0 - 180 ft.

ORANGE TELESTO
Telesto fruticulosa
FAMILY:
Clavulariidae
SUBFAMILY:
Telestinae

SIZE: Colony Height
2 - 6 in.
DEPTH: 75 - 300 ft.

continued next page

Gorgonians

Orange Telesto
Close up.

VISUAL ID: Thick, rubbery, tree-like trunk and branches. Clusters or tufts of polyps on branch tips. Embedded skeletal elements (spicules) visible in translucent trunk and branches. Pastel shades of orange to yellow, gold and pink.

ABUNDANCE & DISTRIBUTION: Rare within safe diving limits Bahamas, Caribbean. Pictured specimens were observed at 120 feet, Cay Sal Banks, Bahamas.

HABITAT & BEHAVIOR: Inhabit deep drop-offs, often under ledge overhangs, wall undercuts and other shaded areas.

Pastel Soft Coral
Close up.

Orange Telesto
continued from previous page

Polyp detail.

PASTEL SOFT CORAL
Neospongodes portoricensis

ORDER:
Alcyonacea
FAMILY:
Nephtheidae

SIZE: Colony Height
$^1/_2$ -1 ft.
DEPTH: 120 - 1650 ft.

IDENTIFICATION GROUP 3

Class Anthozoa
Subclass Hexacorallia

(Hex-ah-core-AL-ee-uh/Gr. & L. six and coral animal)

Hexacorallian polyps are generally smooth and tubular with tentacles in multiples of six. The subclass has six orders that separate anemones, zoanthids, corallimorphs, tube-dwelling anemones (see *Reef Creature Identification),* black corals (see Identification Group 4), and stony corals.

Stony Corals

ORDER Scleractinia (Scler-ak-TIN-ee-uh / L. & Gr. hard and ray)

Stony corals, often called hard corals, are the basic building blocks of tropical coral reefs. These animals (polyps) secrete calcium carbonate to form hard cups, called **corallites,** that provide protection for their soft delicate bodies. In tropical waters most species grow colonially, joining their corallites to produce a substantial structure. Colonies increase in size by asexual budding of additional polyps and successive generations overgrowing one another. The maximum size, shape and design of these structures vary from species to species. Many species can be identified by simply observing the overall structure. Other species, however, grow in similar patterns and require a closer, more detailed inspection of the individual corallites or other parts of the structure before a positive species identification can be made.

Colonial corals that contribute substantial amounts of calcium carbonate (limestone) to the reef structure, are called **hermatypic** or reef-building corals. They live within a narrow temperature range, generally between 70 and 85 degrees Fahrenheit, although most species will survive for short periods, and a few hearty species will grow, in temperatures from 61 to 97 degrees. Non-reef-building corals, called **ahermatypic**, are usually small, occasionally solitary and without substantial skeletons.

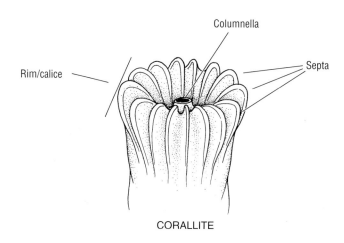

CORALLITE

To assist in the visual identification of stony corals, the 66 species identified in this text have been arranged by the shape and/or appearance of the colony, rather than the traditional scientific family groupings. This method has, in most cases, kept members of the same genus together. The groupings are: (1) **Branching & Pillar Corals**; (2) **Encrusting, Mound & Boulder Corals**; (3) **Brain Corals**; (4) **Leaf, Plate & Sheet Corals**; (5) **Fleshy Corals**; (6) **Cup & Flower Corals**.

BRANCHING & PILLAR CORALS

ENCRUSTING, MOUND & BOULDER CORALS

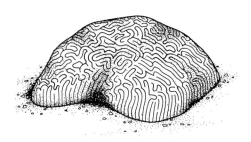

BRAIN CORALS

LEAF, PLATE & SHEET CORALS

FLESHY CORALS

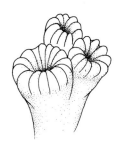

FLOWERING & CUP CORALS

The shape and size of corallites are unique and distinguish species. When colonial structures are similar, close examination of the corallites' structural parts may be required before a correct identification can be made. Generally **corallites** are constructed in a circular pattern, but occasionally they are uneven, oval, Y-shaped or join to form elongated **valleys** and **ridges.** The tubular structure of the polyp's body has a number of vertical infolds on the surface. Calcium carbonate deposited in these folds form thin, upright, radiating plates or ridges, called **septa.** Often the number and structure of the septa are distinctive of species. The corallite structures of many species project above the overall colony forming distinctive rims, called **calices,** which can also be indicative of species. The central axis of a corallite called the **columnella** is below the **polyp mouth.**

The polyps of most Caribbean stony corals are usually retracted into their corallites during the day. At night they extend both their bodies and tentacles for feeding, giving the colony a dramatically different appearance. Their nocturnal form, however, is not useful in determining species. Consequently, only occasional pictures of a coral's nighttime appearance are included in this text.

Reef building corals (hermatypic) typically get their color from single-celled algae, called **zooxanthellae** (zo-zan-THEL-ee), that live in the polyp's tissues. This symbiotic relationship is not fully understood, but clearly the biological processes of each are useful to the other. Most importantly, the zooxanthellae seem to stimulate or aid the secretion of calcium carbonate. Without the algae, coral growth slows dramatically and the polyps' tissues are transparent to translucent revealing the white calcium carbonate skeleton beneath. What causes the algae to be expelled from the polyps' tissues is currently a matter of great scientific concern and debate. It is known that this process, called bleaching, takes place during times of stress; for example, after hurricanes and when water temperatures are unusually high. When conditions return to normal, corals that are bleached regain their zooxanthellae. However, corals cannot live for prolonged periods without the algae. Continued stressful conditions are therefore cause for apprehension. The current fear is that global warming is causing the abnormally high incidence of bleaching and that this may ultimately affect the diversity of corals found on reefs. Non-reef-building corals (ahermatypic) may or may not have zooxanthellae, in which case pigments of their own become prominent. Orange Cup Coral is an example.

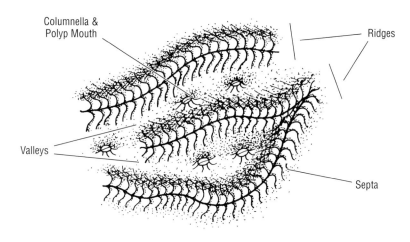

RIDGE-VALLEY

Branching & Pillar Corals

VISUAL ID: Colonies form antler-like racks of cylindrical branches that often grow in great tangles. Surface covered with small, protruding, tubular corallites. Brown to yellow-brown with a single, white terminal corallite. Fragile.

ABUNDANCE & DISTRIBUTION: Occasional to common Bahamas, Caribbean; occasional to uncommon South Florida. Once abundant in many locations throughout the region, but has suffered mass mortality since the early 1990's in many areas due to White-band Disease [pg 244].

HABITAT & BEHAVIOR: Prefer shallow to intermediate depths between 10-60 feet in clear, calm water. Most commonly on reefs, but colonies may grow separately on open clean areas of sand. Often form dense thickets with only outer branches living; the dead interior branches are usually encrusted with algae. Rapidly growing coral; under optimum conditions can grow five to six inches per year. Polyps usually retracted during day.

VISUAL ID: Colonies form antler-like racks of cylindrical branches. Often toward the tips of large branches a spray of shorter branches fuses forming flattened ends similar to Elkhorn Coral [next]; however, the individual branches of the spray remain evident. Surface covered with small, protruding, tubular corallites. Brown to yellow-brown with single, white terminal corallites. Fragile. (Note comparison in photograph, Fused Staghorn on left and Elkhorn on right.)

ABUNDANCE & DISTRIBUTION: Uncommon South Florida, Bahamas, Caribbean. Once abundant in many locations throughout the region, but has suffered mass mortality since the early 1990's in many areas due to White-band Disease [pg 244].

HABITAT & BEHAVIOR: Prefer areas of surge, on fore reefs between 2-12 feet. Rapidly growing coral, under optimum conditions can grow five to six inches per year. Polyps usually retracted during day.

NOTE: New molecular evidence indicates this growth form is a hybrid of Staghorn and Elkhorn Corals.

STAGHORN CORAL
Acropora cervicornis
SUBORDER:
Astrocoeniina
FAMILY:
Acroporidae

SIZE: Colony 1 - 8 ft.
Branch diameter $^3/_4$ - $1^1/_4$ in.
DEPTH: 1 - 160 ft.

Staghorn Coral
*Colonies may cover
large areas.*

Corallite detail.
[far left]

*Tangled colony
over sand.*
[left]

FUSED STAGHORN
Acropora prolifera
SUBORDER:
Astrocoeniina
FAMILY:
Acroporidae

SIZE: Colony 1 - 4 ft.
Branch diameter $^3/_4$ - $1^1/_4$ in.
DEPTH: 1 - 90 ft.

91

Branching & Pillar Corals

VISUAL ID: Colonies form flattened branches resembling the horns of moose or elk. Surface covered with small, protruding, tubular corallites. Brown to yellow-brown. White terminal corallites give the edges of outer branches a white outline. Somewhat fragile, branches break if pressure is applied.

ABUNDANCE & DISTRIBUTION: Common to occasional Bahamas, Caribbean. Once abundant in Florida Keys, but now only occasional. Once abundant in many locations throughout the region, but has suffered mass mortality since the early 1990's in many areas due to White-band Disease [pg 244].

HABITAT & BEHAVIOR: Prefer shallow areas where wave action causes constant water movement. Most common between 1-35 feet. Branches orient parallel to surge direction. Can cover acres of shallow bottom. One of the primary corals of shallow fringing reefs. Upper branches may become exposed at low tide. Rapidly growing coral, under optimum conditions can grow five to six inches per year. Polyps usually retracted during day.

Elkhorn Coral
Corallite detail.

Elkhorn Coral
Colonies growing in shallow unprotected waters, especially on the windward side of fringing reefs, tend to develop rounded stout branches to withstand the force of waves and surge.

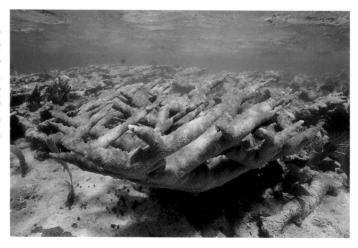

ELKHORN CORAL
Acropora palmata
SUBORDER:
Astrocoeniina
FAMILY:
Acroporidae

SIZE: Colony 3 - 12 ft.
Branch diameter 2 - 10 in.
DEPTH: 1 - 55 ft.

Elkhorn Coral
*Colonies growing
in the shallow
protected lee sides
of fringing reefs
[right]
and those colonies
inhabiting moderate
depth [above]
tend to develop
long, wide flattened
branches.*

Branching & Pillar Corals

VISUAL ID: Colonies form smooth branches with embedded corallites. Colonies grow in several configurations (morphotypes) that were originally described as three separate species. Later because of similarity in corallite structure, most scientists concluded that the morphotypes were variations of one species, caused by different environmental conditions. They were synonymized as one species, Finger Coral, *Porites porites*.

Recent evidence (*Genetic and Morphological Variation in Caribbean and Eastern Pacific Porites,* E. Weil, Proc. 7th. Int. Coral Reef Symposium, Guam, vol. 2: 643-656.) however, strongly indicates there are three separate species. The redescribed scientific and common names follow. (1) **Clubtip Finger Coral,** *P. porites,* has stout, irregular, stubby branches with blunt and often enlarged tips [pictured right]. (2) **Branched Finger Coral,** *P. furcata,* has finger-like, tightly compacted branches. (3) **Thin Finger Coral,** *P. divaricata,* has finger-like, widely spaced branches that often divide near the tip. Color ranges from beige to yellow-brown, brown, gray and gray with purple overtones. Branched and Thin Finger Coral are fragile while Clubtip Finger Coral breaks only under pressure.

ABUNDANCE & DISTRIBUTION: Common to abundant South Florida, Bahamas, Caribbean.

HABITAT & BEHAVIOR: All three morphotypes inhabit most reef environments and depths; however, (1) **Clubtip Finger Coral** is the most common on moderate to deeper reefs; (2) **Branched Finger Coral** frequently forms large beds in shallow back reef areas; (3) **Thin Finger Coral** is most common on shallow back reefs. Polyps are often extended during the day, giving the colony a fuzzy appearance. Brittlestars, sea urchins and chitons often live among the tightly compacted branches of Branched Finger Coral.

(3) Thin Finger Coral
Porites divaricata
Lavender variation.

FINGER CORAL
Porites porites
SUBORDER:
Fungiina
FAMILY:
Poritidae

(1) Clubtip Finger Coral
Porites porites

SIZE: Colony 1 - 4 ft.
Branch diameter
$^1/_2$ - $1^1/_2$ in.
DEPTH: 3 - 160 ft.

(2) Branched Finger Coral
Porites furcata

(3) Thin Finger Coral
Porites divaricata

Branching & Pillar Corals

VISUAL ID: Colonies form numerous, heavy, cylindrical spires that grow upward from an encrusting base mass. Light tan to golden brown and chocolate brown.

ABUNDANCE & DISTRIBUTION: Occasional to rare South Florida, Bahamas, Caribbean.

HABITAT & BEHAVIOR: Inhabit flat and slightly sloping bottoms. Polyps are normally extended during the day, giving colony a fuzzy appearance. Fallen pillars often give rise to several new upward growing pillars.

SIMILAR SPECIES: An unusual growth pattern of Maze Coral *Meandrina meandrites* form *memorialis* [pg.129] appears structurally similar, but the septa pattern of upright plates and ridge grooves is distinctive.

Pillar Coral
Extended polyp detail.

PILLAR CORAL
Dendrogyra cylindrus
SUBORDER:
Faviina
FAMILY:
Meandrinidae

SIZE: Colony 4 - 10 ft.
Pillar diameter 3 - 5 in.
DEPTH: 4 - 65 ft.

Pillar Coral
*Fallen colony growing
new upright pillars.*

Mature colony.
[far left]

Young colony.
[left]

Branching & Pillar Corals

VISUAL ID: Colonies form small, densely branching clumps in shallow water. Deeper, in depths generally over 65 feet, branching becomes more widely spaced. Branches have fine ridges running their length, and each ends with a single corallite. Tan to golden brown and dark brown. Fragile.

ABUNDANCE & DISTRIBUTION: Common to occasional Florida, Bahamas, Caribbean.

HABITAT & BEHAVIOR: Most commonly inhabit shallow areas of high sedimentation, such as Turtle Grass beds [pg.191]. Rarely on clear water reefs. Much of the colony is often dead, and may be covered with sediment, with only polyps at tips of outer branches living.

NOTE: Also commonly known as "Ivory Tube Coral." Formerly classified in Suborder Faviina, Family Faviidae.

Tube Coral

Deep water variation; note widely spread branches.

VISUAL ID: Colonies form large, bushy or tree-like structures. Colony base (trunk) can be quite thick, branches long and tapering. Only corallites' rims protrude from colony. (Similar Diffuse Ivory Bush Coral, Delicate Bush Ivory Coral and Large Ivory Coral [next three species] distinguished by prominently protruding corallites.) Yellowish brown. Thin branch tips fragile.

ABUNDANCE & DISTRIBUTION: Abundant West Florida. Absent East Florida, Bahamas, Caribbean.

HABITAT & BEHAVIOR: Inhabit areas of hard substrate.

NOTE: Photographed specimen collected and visual identification confirmed by magnified examination of corallites and structure.

TUBE CORAL
Cladocora arbuscula
SUBORDER:
Caryophylliina
FAMILY:
Caryophylliidae

SIZE: Colony 1 - 6 in.
Corallite diameter ¹/₄ in.
DEPTH: 3 - 65 ft.

Tube Coral
*Corallites protruding
from sand in
turtle grass bed.*

ROBUST IVORY TREE CORAL
Oculina robusta
SUBORDER:
Faviina
FAMILY:
Oculinidae

SIZE: Colony 4 - 30 in.
Corallite diameter ¹/₄ in.
Branch diameter to 3 in.
DEPTH: 20 - 85 ft.

VISUAL ID: Colonies form small clumps of thin branches. Branches may occasionally cross and fuse. Corallites protrude prominently from sides of branches. Branch diameter, corallite diameter and length all nearly equal. Cream to white. Fragile. Ahermatypic and often without zooxanthellae.

ABUNDANCE & DISTRIBUTION: Uncommon West Florida; rare East Florida. Not reported Bahamas, Caribbean.

HABITAT & BEHAVIOR: Inhabit areas of rocky rubble, shell hash under ledge overhangs and shipwrecks.

NOTE: Photographed specimen collected (USNM 91649) and visual identification confirmed by magnified examination of corallites and structure.

VISUAL ID: Colonies form densely branched, thicket-like clumps. Branches tend to be short, are often crooked and bear numerous raised corallites. Yellow-brown, but often encrusted with organisms of different color. Somewhat fragile and may lack zooxanthellae.

ABUNDANCE & DISTRIBUTION: Abundant to occasional Florida; common to occasional Bahamas; occasional to rare Caribbean. Absent around some islands, especially in northwest and southern Caribbean.

HABITAT & BEHAVIOR: Generally inhabit shallow water areas of high sedimentation, including sloping solid bottoms, reefs, back reefs and lagoons. Often attach to old shipwrecks. Much of the colony is often dead, and may be covered with sediment. Rarely deeper than 40 feet.

SIMILAR SPECIES: Ivory Tree Coral, *O. valenciennesi,* distinguished by longer, more tree-like branches, corallite rims low, often sunken into the branch structure. Common in Bermuda; rare or absent Florida, Bahamas, Caribbean.

Diffuse Ivory Bush Coral

Colony with branches lacking zooxanthellae and others with lavender pigmentation.

DELICATE IVORY BUSH CORAL
Oculina tenella
SUBORDER:
Faviina
FAMILY:
Oculinidae

SIZE: Colony 1 - 4 in.
Corallite diameter $^1/_8$ in.
Branch diameter to $^1/_4$ in.
DEPTH: 60 - 250 ft.

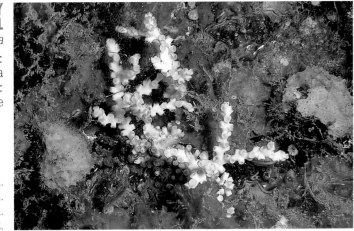

DIFFUSE IVORY BUSH CORAL
Oculina diffusa
SUBORDER:
Faviina
FAMILY:
Oculinidae

SIZE: Colony 1 - 12 in.
Corallite diameter $^1/_4$ in.
Branch diameter to $^1/_2$ in.
DEPTH: 3 - 75 ft.

Diffuse Ivory Bush Coral
Colony on dark interior ceiling of shipwreck lacks zooxanthellae.

(USNM 92075)

101

VISUAL ID: Colonies form large, tangled clumps of long crooked branches. Corallites extend prominently from raised mounds on branches' sides, except on smaller branches and near branch tips. Yellowish brown; without zooxanthellae, white to lavender. Thinner branches fragile.

ABUNDANCE & DISTRIBUTION: Uncommon Florida; rare to absent Bahamas, Caribbean.

HABITAT & BEHAVIOR: Wide range of habitats from shallow reefs to deep, rocky outcroppings. Rare in shallow water, most common between 150-300 feet. Small colonies not uncommon, 75-125 feet, central and northern Florida Atlantic Coast.

NOTE: Photographed specimens collected (USNM 91669) and visual identification confirmed by magnified examination of corallites and structure.

Large Ivory Coral
Small colony.

(USNM 91670)

VISUAL ID: Colonies form densely packed clumps of small pencil-sized branches with blunt tips. Colonies appear fuzzy when polyps are extended. Creamy to bright yellow. Fragile.

ABUNDANCE & DISTRIBUTION: Common South Florida, Bahamas, Caribbean.

HABITAT & BEHAVIOR: Generally inhabit deeper, clear water, outer reefs. Occasionally in shallower water with some sedimentation and water movement. Often cover considerable area of flat bottom. Polyps are generally extended.

SIMILAR SPECIES: Pointed Pencil Coral, *M. asperula,* branches tapered rather than blunt. A deep dwelling azooxanthellate coral known primarily from the southern Caribbean.

NOTE: Also commonly known as "Small Finger Coral" and "Branching Coral." Formerly classified in Family Pocilloporidae.

LARGE IVORY CORAL
Oculina varicosa
SUBORDER:
Faviina
FAMILY:
Oculinidae

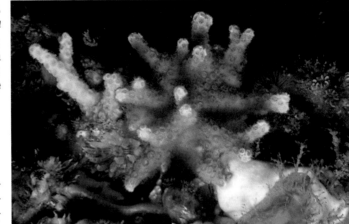

SIZE: Colony 3 - 24 in.
Corallite diameter ¹/₄ in.
Branch diameter ¹/₂ - 2 in.
DEPTH: 15 - 300 ft.

Large Ivory Coral
Branch detail:
note corallites'
swollen bases.

YELLOW PENCIL CORAL
Madracis mirabilis
SUBORDER:
Astrocoeniina
FAMILY:
Astrocoeniidae

SIZE: Colony 5 in. - 4 ft.
Branch diameter ¹/₄ - ³/₈ in.
DEPTH: 3 - 190 ft.

continued next page

Yellow Pencil Coral
Small colony with polyps extended.

VISUAL ID: Colonies form densely packed clumps of thick, relatively short branches with blunt and occasionally expanded and double-lobed tips. Corallites have eight septa (rays). Colonies appear fuzzy when polyps are extended. Tan to yellow-brown, yellow-green, brown and green; polyp's mouth yellow. Not fragile, but will break under moderate pressure.

ABUNDANCE & DISTRIBUTION: Common to occasional South Florida, Bahamas, Caribbean.

HABITAT & BEHAVIOR: Inhabit deep outer reefs, often on outcroppings and ledges along walls.

NOTE: Also commonly known as "Branching Cactus Coral." Formerly classified in Family Pocilloporidae.

Eight-ray Finger Coral
Corallite detail.

Yellow Pencil Coral

continued from previous page

Branch detail; note blunt tips.

EIGHT-RAY FINGER CORAL

Madracis formosa

SUBORDER:
Astrocoeniina
FAMILY:
Astrocoeniidae

SIZE: Colony 1 - 5 ft.
Branch diameter $^3/_4$ - $1^1/_4$ in.
DEPTH: 60 - 200 ft.

Eight-ray Finger Coral

Small colony.

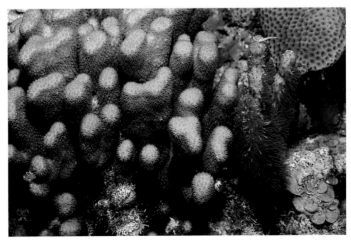

Encrusting, Mound & Boulder Corals

VISUAL ID: Thinly encrusting, small colonies, often with raised, tightly bunched lobes or knobs. Surface densely covered with separated, small, protruding corallites with ten septa (rays). Often green, but vary from yellow-brown to violet-brown, tan and gray.

ABUNDANCE & DISTRIBUTION: Common South Florida, Bahamas, Caribbean.

HABITAT & BEHAVIOR: Inhabit most reef environments. Usually develop lobes and knobs when growing in the open and exposed to bright light. Form irregular encrustations in shaded, protected areas of reef, under ledge overhangs and on deep walls.

NOTE: Encrusting variation is visually indistinguishable from Encrusting Star Coral, *M. pharensis* form *luciphila* [next page], but can usually be identified by habitat. Positive identification requires magnified examination of specimen sample. Ten-Ray Star Coral has ten primary septa, while Encrusting Star Coral has ten primary and ten secondary septa and small lobes around the columella. Identification of pictured specimens was confirmed by examination of small collected samples. Formerly classified in Family Pocilloporidae.

Ten-ray Star Coral
Large encrusting colony on deep wall.

VISUAL ID: Thick encrusting colonies that generally conform to the contours of the substrate. Cylindrical corallites are closely spaced and noticeably larger that those of similar appearing species in the genus. Readily distinguished by its six septa around the edge of the corallite that extend well above the cup structure as rounded lobes. Green to chocolate brown.

ABUNDANCE & DISTRIBUTION: Occasional Bahamas, Caribbean.

HABITAT & BEHAVIOR: Inhabit most deep reef environments, most common below 70 feet. Formerly classified in Family Pocilloporidae.

TEN-RAY STAR CORAL
Madracis decactis
SUBORDER:
Astrocoeniina
FAMILY:
Astrocoeniidae

SIZE: Colony 1 - 6 in.
Lobe diameter about 1 in.
DEPTH: 5 - 130 ft.

Ten-ray Star Coral
*Corallite detail; knobby
and encrusting variation.*

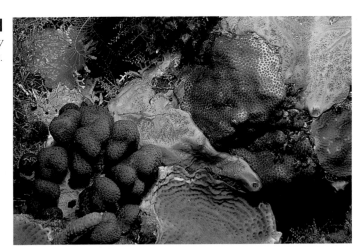

SIX-RAY STAR CORAL
Madracis senaria
SUBORDER:
Astrocoeniina
FAMILY:
Astrocoeniidae

SIZE: Colony 1 - 2 ft.
DEPTH: 50 - 130 ft.

VISUAL ID: Colonies grow in two forms. Form *pharensis* [right] is either thinly encrusting, spreading in long ribbons, or may form numerous small knobs. May be shades of cream, yellow, pale green, dull red, pink or lavender. Ahermatypic. Form *luciphila* is thickly encrusting and may have a smooth or somewhat lumpy surface. Green to brown or gray. Hermatypic.

ABUNDANCE & DISTRIBUTION: Occasional Bahamas, Caribbean. Not reported Florida.

HABITAT & BEHAVIOR: Form *pharensis* grows in dark areas, such as the underside of plate corals and cave ceilings; most common deeper than 60 feet. Form *luciphila* generally grows in exposed, well lighted areas of reef, often encrusting the sheer faces of cliffs, canyon and drop-off walls; may be as shallow as six feet.

NOTE: Form *luciphila* is visually indistinguishable from the encrusting variation of Ten-ray Star Coral [see previous note]. There is evidence suggesting that Encrusting Star Coral is a form of Ten-ray Star Coral. (See D. Fenner, *Bull.Mar.Sci.*, Vol. 53, No. 3, 1993.) Identification confirmed by examination of collected samples.

VISUAL ID: Colonies form thick encrustations over areas of dead coral and rocky substrate. Extended polyps give colony soft, fuzzy appearance. When polyps are retracted, small, pitted, polygonal corallites give colony porous appearance. Pale bluish to greenish or whitish. Easily confused with Massive and Lesser Starlet Corals [pg. 123]. but can be be distinguished by color and shape of corallite pits.

ABUNDANCE & DISTRIBUTION: Occasional southern Caribbean. Not reported Florida, Bahamas and balance of Caribbean.

HABITAT & BEHAVIOR: Inhabit shallow, dead areas of older reefs. Often in back reef areas of sand, coral rubble and coral heads.

NOTE: An undescribed species similar to *Porites branneri* found in Brazilian waters.

STAR CORAL
Madracis pharensis
SUBORDER:
Astrocoeniina
FAMILY:
Pocilloporidae

Form *pharensis*

SIZE: Colony 1 - 6 in.
DEPTH: 6 - 450 ft.

Star Coral
Form pharensis,
knobby variation
on deep cave ceiling.

Encrusting Star Coral
Form luciphila,
encrusting shallow reef.
[far left]

Encrusting shallow
canyon wall . [left]

BLUE CRUST CORAL
Porites sp.
SUBORDER:
Fungiina
FAMILY:
Poritidae

SIZE: Colony 2 - 6 in.
DEPTH: 1 - 35 ft.

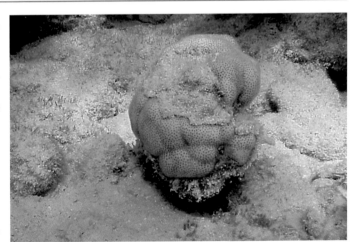

Encrusting, Mound & Boulder Corals

VISUAL ID: Colonies form relatively smooth domes or boulders; occasionally encrust substrate. Circular, upper rims of calices darker than surrounding area. Brownish-cream to tan, brown and gray. Corallites may be widely spaced or closely compacted. When approached or touched appear to "blush" a lighter shade. (This is caused by the rapid retraction of its tiny, normally extended polyps.)

ABUNDANCE & DISTRIBUTION: Occasional South Florida, Bahamas, Caribbean.

HABITAT & BEHAVIOR: Inhabit most reef environments. Numerous reddish Blushing Star Coral Fanworms, *Vermiliopsos* n. sp., [Reef Creature ID] often associate with this species. When present, they retract with the polyps, enhancing the blushing effect.

NOTE: Visual identification of pictured specimens confirmed by collection of small samples and magnified examination of corallites. Formerly classified as species *michelinii*.

Blushing Star Coral
Encrusting variation, polyps extended.

Blushing Star Coral
Tightly compacted polyp variation; note fanworms.

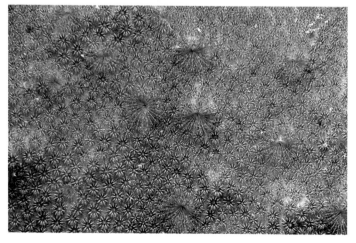

BLUSHING STAR CORAL
Stephanocoenia intersepta
SUBORDER:
Astrocoeniina
FAMILY:
Astrocoeniidae

SIZE: Colony ¹/₂ - 2¹/₂ ft.
DEPTH: 10 - 130 ft.

Blushing Star Coral
Detail: encrusting variation,
polyps retracted.

(USNM 92955)

Blushing Star Coral
Boulder variation with tightly
compacted polyps.

(USNM 92954)

Encrusting, Mound & Boulder Corals

VISUAL ID: (1) **Lobed Star Coral,** *M. annularis* [right], grow in clusters of long, thick columns with enlarged, dome-like tops. Living polyps are restricted to the upper portions of the column, while lower parts are often bioeroded and fouled with algae. Surfaces are usually smooth with close, uniformly distributed and evenly extended corallites. (2) **Mountainous Star Coral,** *M. faveolata*, grow in large, massive mounds [below left] and sheets with skirt-like edges [right middle]. Often cone-like bumps form on the surface that are usually arranged in vertical rows. Surfaces are usually smooth with uniformly distributed and evenly extended corallites. (3) **Boulder Star Coral,** *M. franksi* [right bottom], grow in irregular mounds and encrustations with scattered lumps. Surfaces are rough with unevenly distributed and extended corallites. Often small clusters of polyps are without zooxanthellae. (4) One and possibly two deepwater morphotypes of flattened plates (some smooth, others lumpy), often stacked in shingle-like fashion [below right], require further investigation to determine the appropriate classification. All types vary in shades of green to brown, yellow-brown and gray.

ABUNDANCE & DISTRIBUTION: Common to abundant South Florida, Bahamas, Caribbean.

HABITAT & BEHAVIOR: Growth configurations (1), (2) and (3) inhabit most reef environments and together are often the predominate coral between 20-75 feet. Of the three, (2) is generally the most common. Flattened plate morphtypes (4) usually grow at depths greater than 80 feet.

BOULDER STAR CORAL
Montastraea annularis

SUBORDER:
Faviina
FAMILY:
Faviidae

(1) Lobed Star Coral
Montastraea annularis

SIZE: Colony 1 - 10 ft.
Corallites diameter ⅛ in.
DEPTH: 6 - 130 ft.

(2) Mountainous Star Coral
Montastraea faveolata

(3) Boulder Star Coral
Montastraea franksi
[below right]

*Colony and corallite detail;
note occasional polyps
without zooxanthellae.*
[below left]

(1) Mountainous Star Coral
[left – pg. 112]

(4) Flat Plate Morphotype
[right – pg. 112]

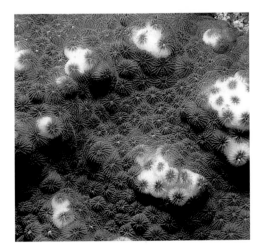

Encrusting, Mound & Boulder Corals

VISUAL ID: Colonies usually form massive boulders and domes, but occasionally develop into plates or sheets, especially in deep water. Surface is covered with distinctive, blister-like corallites. Shades of green, brown, yellow-brown and gray. Occasionally fluoresce red or orange. (Fluorescence is not visible when lit by a hand light or strobe.)

ABUNDANCE & DISTRIBUTION: Common to abundant South Florida, Bahamas, Caribbean.

HABITAT & BEHAVIOR: Inhabit most reef environments and are often the predominant coral between 40-100 feet. Polyps are generally retracted during the day, but extend prominently at night.

NOTE: Also commonly known as "Large Star Coral."

Great Star Coral
Reef top colony.

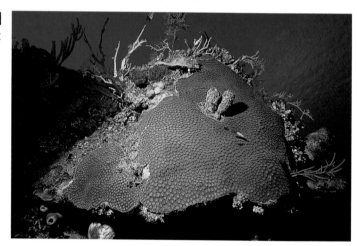

Great Star Coral
Extended polyp detail.

GREAT STAR CORAL
Montastraea cavernosa
SUBORDER:
Faviina
FAMILY:
Faviidae

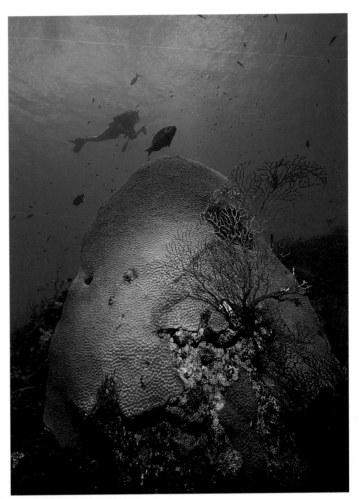

SIZE: Colony 2 - 8 ft.
Corallites diameter ¹/₄ - ¹/₂ in.
DEPTH: 6 - 300 ft.

Great Star Coral
Corallite detail.

VISUAL ID: Colonies form relatively smooth domes, occasionally with a few slight, irregular bulges on their surfaces. Corallite rims protrude noticeably, giving a blistered appearance. Cream to light tan; extended polyps light tan to brown.

ABUNDANCE & DISTRIBUTION: Common to occasional South Florida; uncommon Bahamas, Caribbean.

HABITAT & BEHAVIOR: Inhabit reefs from shallow to moderate depths.

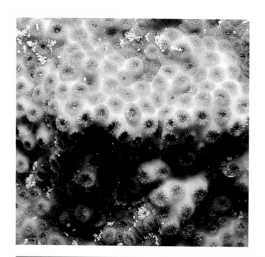 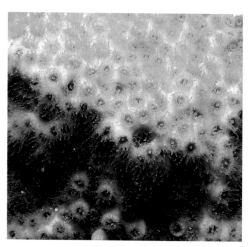

VISUAL ID: Colonies form lobated heads with irregular bulges on the surface. Corallite rims protrude noticeably and are irregularly spaced, some almost touching, while others may be separated by as much as their diameter. Usually yellow-brown, occasionally cream to tan; polyps dark brown.

ABUNDANCE & DISTRIBUTION: Abundant to occasional Florida; occasional to rare Bahamas, Caribbean.

HABITAT & BEHAVIOR: Inhabit a wide range of underwater environments from areas of high sedimentation, including back reefs, lagoons and Turtle Grass beds [pg. 191] to deep outer reefs. Can tolerate cool water; grow as far north as North Carolina where winter water temperatures may fall below 50°F.

NOTE: Also commonly known as "Stump Coral," "Lobed Star Coral" and "Eyed Coral."

SMOOTH STAR CORAL
Solenastrea bournoni
SUBORDER:
Faviina
FAMILY:
Faviidae

SIZE: Colony 4 - 18 in.
DEPTH: 5 - 60 ft.

Smooth Star Coral
Colony in natural light.

Corallite detail.
[far left]

Polyp detail.
[left]

KNOBBY STAR CORAL
Solenastrea hyades
SUBORDER:
Faviina
FAMILY:
Faviidae

SIZE: Colony 3 in. - 2 ft.
DEPTH: 2 - 60 ft.

continued next page

VISUAL ID: Colonies form rounded heads, domes and flattened plates. Corallites protrude perceptibly (up to one-quarter inch) and are usually elliptical or circular and occasionally Y-shaped. Cream to yellow and brown.

ABUNDANCE & DISTRIBUTION: Common Bahamas and Caribbean; occasional South Florida.

HABITAT & BEHAVIOR: Inhabit most reef environments. Most common between 30-80 feet. Rarely on reef crests.

NOTE: The flattened plate variation was formerly known as "Pancake Star Coral" and classified as a separate species, *D. stellaris,* but is now considered synonymous with *D. stokesi.* The rounded head variation is also commonly known as "Pineapple Star Coral."

Knobby Star Coral
continued from previous page

Colony on reef.

Small colony detail.
[left]

Colony in turtle grass.
[far left]

ELLIPTICAL STAR CORAL
Dichocoenia stokesi

SUBORDER:
Faviina
FAMILY:
Meandrinidae

SIZE: Colony 4 - 15 in.
DEPTH: 12 - 225 ft.

Elliptical Star Coral
Flattened plate variation.

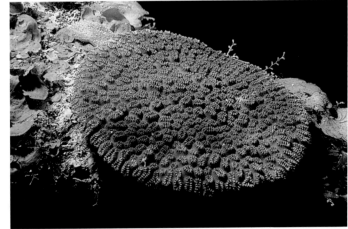

Polyp/corallite detail.
[far left]

Rounded head variation.
[left]

VISUAL ID: Usually form small hemispherical domes, but occasionally encrust small areas of substrate. Corallites are generally oval with protruding rims. Yellow to golden-brown and brown. (Easily distinguished from similar Elliptical Star Coral, *Dichocoenia stokesi*, [previous] by colonies' smaller size and less pronounced protrusion of corallites.)

ABUNDANCE & DISTRIBUTION: Common Florida, Bahamas, Caribbean.

HABITAT & BEHAVIOR: Inhabit shallow reefs and rocky substrates. Most common between 10-40 feet.

NOTE: Also commonly known as "Star Coral."

VISUAL ID: Colonies encrust in shallow, surging water, but form rounded heads and domes in deeper water. Surface lumpy and covered with small, closely set corallites that give the colonies a porous appearance. Most commonly yellow to yellow-green or yellow-brown, occasionally beige to gray. Extended polyps give colonies a soft, fuzzy appearance. A rare cryptic thin plate form often mixing with lettuce and sheet corals can be confused with Honeycomb Plate Coral, *P. colonensis* [pg. 135]

ABUNDANCE & DISTRIBUTION: Abundant to common Florida, Bahamas, Caribbean.

HABITAT & BEHAVIOR: Inhabit all reef environments. Most common between 15-80 feet. Polyps usually extended.

NOTE: Also commonly known as "Yellow Porous Coral" and "Porous Coral."

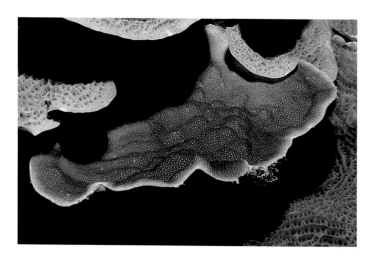

GOLFBALL CORAL
Favia fragum
SUBORDER:
Faviina
FAMILY:
Faviidae

SIZE: Colony 1 - 2 in.
DEPTH: 3 - 90 ft.

MUSTARD HILL CORAL
Porites astreoides
SUBORDER:
Fungiina
FAMILY:
Poritidae

SIZE: Colony 6 in. - 2 ft.
DEPTH: 3 - 160 ft.

Mustard Hill Coral
Gray variation.

Polyp detail.
[far left]

*Rare cryptic plate
form and color.*
[left]

VISUAL ID: Form rounded heads, boulders or domes. Surface covered with small, generally symmetrically round, pitted corallites. Light gray to golden-brown and brown; color uniform, corallites not dark at center. Young colonies are small, encrusting and difficult to distinguish from Lesser Starlet Coral [next] that have corallites less symmetrically round, more deeply pitted with dark centers, and more pronounced septa.

ABUNDANCE & DISTRIBUTION: Common Florida, Bahamas, Caribbean.

HABITAT & BEHAVIOR: Tend to inhabit shallow to moderate reefs, between 25-45 feet. Prefer clear water. Generally in protected areas of shallower reefs and all deeper reef environments. Usually deeper than similar Lesser Starlet Coral, *Siderastrea radians*, [next].

NOTE: Also commonly known as "Smooth Starlet," "Round Starlet," and "Reef Starlet Coral."

**Massive
Starlet Coral**
*Corallite detail comparison:
Massive Starlet (left),
Lesser Starlet. (right).*

VISUAL ID: Colonies usually form flat, encrusting plates, but occasionally grow in small, irregular and rounded domes. In shallow water they may form unattached, egg-shaped colonies that are rolled freely across the bottom by surge. Surface is covered with small, deep-pitted corallites that often appear "pinched-in". Usually whitish to light gray, occasionally light tan; center of corallite appears dark. Can be confused with Massive Starlet Coral [previous] that have corallites less steeply sloped, not dark toward center, and septa less pronounced, and with Blue Crust Coral [pg. 109].

ABUNDANCE & DISTRIBUTION: Common Florida, Bahamas, Caribbean.

HABITAT & BEHAVIOR: Inhabit flat rocky/sandy substrates, most commonly from low tide line to 20 feet, also shallow reefs and back reefs. Rarely below 30 feet. Can tolerate surge, sandy, silty conditions and temperature fluctuations. Usually shallower than similar Massive Starlet [previous].

NOTE: Also commonly known as "Rough Starlet," "Starlet Coral,"and "Shallow-water Starlet Coral."

MASSIVE STARLET CORAL
Siderastrea siderea

SUBORDER:
Fungiina
FAMILY:
Siderastreidae

SIZE: Colony 1 - 6 ft.
DEPTH: 2 - 220 ft.

Massive Starlet Coral
Dome variation.

LESSER STARLET CORAL
Siderastrea radians

SUBORDER:
Fungiina
FAMILY:
Siderastreidae

SIZE: Colony 4 - 12 in.
DEPTH: 0 - 90 ft.

Brain Corals

VISUAL ID: Colonies form smoothly contoured plates to hemispherical domes. Long valleys are often connected and usually convoluted, except near colony's edge. Ridges evenly rounded, usually without a top groove, although occasionally with an extremely fine groove, especially near colony edge. (Similar Boulder Brain Coral [pg. 133] has a distinct groove on top of ridge. Similar Knobby Brain Coral [next] distinguished by sharply raised ridges and knobby surface.) Green to brown, yellow-brown and bluish gray; valleys often lighter or of contrasting color.

ABUNDANCE & DISTRIBUTION: Abundant to common Florida, Bahamas, Caribbean.

HABITAT & BEHAVIOR: Inhabit many marine environments, most common between 20-40 feet.

NOTE: Also commonly known as "Common Brain Coral," and "Smooth Brain Coral."

VISUAL ID: Colonies form hemispherical domes or encrust rocky substrate. Surfaces of colonies usually have numerous, irregular knobs, but occasionally form smooth low, flattened domes. Ridges rise sharply and do not have a groove on top. (Similar Boulder Brain Coral [pg. 133] has a distinct groove on ridge top. Similar Symmetrical Brain Coral [previous] distinguished by evenly rounded ridges and smooth contour of colony.) Green to brown, yellow-brown and bluish gray; valleys often lighter or of contrasting color.

ABUNDANCE & DISTRIBUTION: Common Florida, Bahamas, Caribbean.

HABITAT & BEHAVIOR: Inhabit many shallow environments, including both seaward and lagoon sides of reefs, Turtle Grass beds [pg. 191] and even on mangrove roots. Most common between 3-20 feet.

NOTE: Also commonly known as "Encrusting Brain Coral," "Sharp-hilled Brain Coral."

SYMMETRICAL BRAIN CORAL
Diploria strigosa

SUBORDER:
Faviina
FAMILY:
Faviidae

SIZE: Colony 6 in. - 6 ft.
DEPTH: 3 - 130 ft.

Symmetrical Brain Coral

Hemispherical head variation.

Structural detail; note evenly rounded ridges.
[far left]

Encrusting plate variation.
[left]

KNOBBY BRAIN CORAL
Diploria clivosa

SUBORDER:
Faviina
FAMILY:
Faviidae

SIZE: Colony 6 in. - 4 ft.
DEPTH: 3 - 135 ft.

continued next page

Brain Corals

Knobby Brain Coral

Structural detail; note steep ridges.

VISUAL ID: Colonies form hemispherical heads. Deep, often narrow, polyp bearing valleys are separated by broad ridges with wide, conspicuous trough-like grooves. Width and depth of grooves vary greatly from colony to colony, but are always obvious and usually make the ridge appear as two. Valleys are highly convoluted and often interconnected. Tan to yellow-brown to brown to brownish gray.

ABUNDANCE & DISTRIBUTION: Common to occasional South Florida, Bahamas, Caribbean.

HABITAT & BEHAVIOR: Inhabit seaward slope of reefs. Most common between 15-50 feet. Tentacle tips are often visible in the narrow valleys during the day.

NOTE: Also commonly known as "Depressed Brain Coral" and "Labyrinthine Brain Coral."

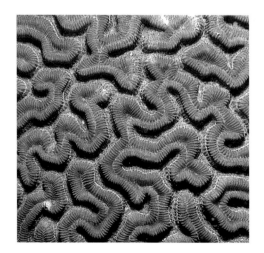

Knobby Brain Coral
continued from previous page

Encrusting variation.

GROOVED BRAIN CORAL
Diploria labyrinthiformis
SUBORDER:
Faviina
FAMILY:
Faviidae

SIZE: Colony 1 - 4 ft.
DEPTH: 3 - 135 ft.

Grooved Brain Coral
Colony with unusually wide grooves.

Structural detail comparing different groove widths.
[left & far left]

127

Brain Corals

VISUAL ID: Colonies form both hemispherical heads and flattened plates. Ridges are created by smooth, widely separated, vertical plates (septa). There is a thin line along ridge tops where plates come together. Tan to yellow-brown and brown. There are three additional growth patterns; both form small elliptical colonies with cone-shaped undersides, often with short central stalks. Form *danai* has a long, continuous, central valley and opposing side valleys. The central valley divides into two branches at the ends. Form *brasiliensis* does not divide into two branches at ends and may not have a continuous central valley. Form *memorialis* grow in columns resembling Pillar Coral [pg. 97].

ABUNDANCE & DISTRIBUTION: Common to occasional South Florida, Bahamas, Caribbean.

HABITAT & BEHAVIOR: Inhabit most reef environments, especially on seaward reefs at depths between 25-75 feet. F. *danae* and f. *brasiliensis* often in areas of coral rubble and sand and may not be firmly attached to substrate.

NOTE: Also commonly known as "Butterprint Brain Coral" and "Tan Brain Coral."

Maze Coral
Brazilian Rose Coral
form brasiliensis,
without central valley.

MAZE CORAL
Meandrina meandrites
SUBORDER:
Faviina
FAMILY:
Meandrinidae

SIZE: Colony 1 - 3 ft.
DEPTH: 2 - 240 ft.

Maze Coral
*Plate-like variation
at night with
polyps extended.*

*Maze Coral hemispherical
head variation.*
[left]

*Butterprint Pillar Coral
form* memorialis.
[far left]

Maze Coral
*Butterprint Rose Coral
form* danai;
*note central valley
and branched ends.*

Brain Corals

VISUAL ID: Colonies grow in two patterns. The most common builds small elliptical colonies with long, continuous central valley and several short side valleys. Cone-shaped underside, often with short central stalk. The second pattern builds hemispherical heads with winding valleys and ridges and flattish underside. Brown to yellow-brown, gray or green. Ridges and valleys often of contrasting shades or different color. (Distinguished from similar appearing forms of Maze Coral [previous] by less pronounced vertical plates.) Often young colonies form small circular to oval disks that can be confused with similar appearing Solitary Disk Coral [pg.157].

ABUNDANCE & DISTRIBUTION: Common to uncommon Florida, Bahamas, Caribbean.

HABITAT & BEHAVIOR: The small elliptical colonies tend to inhabit areas of coral rubble, sand and Turtle Grass [pg. 191], and are often unattached. The hemispherical heads tend to inhabit reefs along with other stony corals, and are attached.

NOTE: Some scientists consider the hemispherical head pattern a separate species or *form mayori* and is commonly known as "Tortugas Rose Coral."

Rose Coral
Colony in turtle grass bed, tentacles extended.

Rose Coral
Tortugas Rose Coral form mayori *hemispherical head growth pattern.*

ROSE CORAL
Manicina areolata
SUBORDER:
Faviina
FAMILY:
Faviidae

SIZE: Elliptical
Colony 2 - 6 in.
Hemispherical
Colony 4 - 8 in.
DEPTH: 2 - 200 ft.

Rose Coral
*Tortugas Rose Coral
form* mayori
*hemispherical head
growth pattern.*

Rose Coral
*Young disk-shaped
colony.*

(USNM 92082)

Brain Corals – Leaf, Plate & Sheet Corals

VISUAL ID: Colonies generally form large rounded domes, but also encrust, constructing large rounded plates. Surface covered with a convoluted system of ridges and valleys. A thin, but distinct groove runs along the ridge tops. There is also a thin, but noticeable line approximately halfway down the ridge where the slope decreases in angle and slants to form the valley. Typically the ridges are brown and valleys green, tan or whitish. Valleys are usually long and meandering, containing several polyps, but are occasionally closed, holding only one or two polyps.

ABUNDANCE & DISTRIBUTION: Common South Florida, Bahamas, Caribbean.

HABITAT & BEHAVIOR: Generally inhabit reef tops and seaward reef slopes. Most common between 20-80 feet. Polyps are extended only at night, their tentacles forming long meandering rows along the ridges (below).

NOTE: Colonies composed primarily of closed valleys were formerly known as "Closed-valley Brain Coral" and classified as a separate species, *C. breviserialis,* but are now synonymous with *C. natans.* Also commonly known as "Giant Brain Coral."

BOULDER BRAIN CORAL
Colpophyllia natans
SUBORDER:
Faviina
FAMILY:
Faviidae

SIZE: Colony 1¹/₂ - 7 ft.
DEPTH: 2 - 175 ft.

Boulder Brain Coral
Colony with closed-valleys.

*Young colony
can be confused with
Ridged Cactus Coral,*
Mycetophylia lamarkiana
pg. 149. [far left]

Close valley detail. [left]

Boulder Brain Coral
Massive colony.

Polyps partially extended.
[far left]

Polyps retracted.
[left]

VISUAL ID: Colonies form thin plates that encrust and contour over the substrate, occasionally with lumpy surfaces. Colonies' edges extend outward from substrate, are often undulated and generally rounded. May form in overlapping, shingle-like plates. Polyps are dark brown to greenish brown with bright white contrasting centers that distinguish them from similar appearing coral colonies; on occasion the polyps are red with contrasting green centers.

ABUNDANCE & DISTRIBUTION: Occasional to uncommon Central American coast and offshore islands from Panama to Yucatan and probably the entire Caribbean.

HABITAT & BEHAVIOR: Inhabit sloping reef faces, attaching to and encrusting the rocky substrate; also reported to overgrow sponges and areas of algae.

NOTE: This species was first described in 1990; its distribution and abundance are not well documented. Some scientists consider this species a form of Mustard Hill Coral, *P. astreoides* [pg.121].

VISUAL ID: Colonies form saucers or plates with distinctive thin lines (septa) running toward the edges. Occasionally grow in overlapping shingle-like style. Ridges and valleys are not continuous. Corallite centers are distinctively nestled in rows against ridges' steep outer edges. Inner ridge faces slope more gently toward colonies' centers. Tan to yellow-brown, brown and gray; may fluoresce green, blue or purple tints. Fragile.

ABUNDANCE & DISTRIBUTION: Common to occasional South Florida, Bahamas, Caribbean.

HABITAT & BEHAVIOR: Inhabit sloping reef faces and along walls. Most common between 25-100 feet.

NOTE: Also commonly known as "Saucer Coral," "Sunray Plate Coral" and "Fragile Lettuce Coral." Formerly reported as *Leptoseris cucullata*.

Sunray Lettuce Coral
Detail: note corallites nestled in rows against ridges' steep outer edges.

HONEYCOMB PLATE CORAL
Porites colonensis
SUBORDER:
Fungiina
FAMILY:
Poritidae

SIZE: Colony 6 - 18 in.
DEPTH: 10 - 90 ft.

SUNRAY LETTUCE CORAL
Helioseris cucullata
SUBORDER:
Fungiina
FAMILY:
Agariciidae

SIZE: Colony 4 - 10 in.
DEPTH: 10 - 280 ft.

Sunray Lettuce Coral
*Overlapping,
shingle-like pattern.*

VISUAL ID: Colonies form small, thin saucer-like colonies. Ridges and long continuous valleys form an uneven pattern of concentric circles radiating from center of colony. The ridges of deep water colonies are often low and inconspicuous. Polyps are only present in the valleys of the upper surface; the underside is quite smooth. Shades of purplish brown, chocolate, yellow-brown, tan, and greenish tan. Fragile. Form *contracta* colonies have pinched corallites and often grow in irregular, occasionally gnarled patterns.

ABUNDANCE & DISTRIBUTION: Occasional Florida, Bahamas, Caribbean.

HABITAT & BEHAVIOR: Inhabit sloping reef faces, under ledge overhangs and along walls.

NOTE: Visual identification of the two colonies on bottom of these pages confirmed by collection and magnified examination.

Fragile Saucer Coral
Low profile ridge chocolate variation.

Fragile Saucer Coral
Low profile ridge, yellow-brown variation.

(USNM 92094)

136

FRAGILE SAUCER CORAL
Agaricia fragilis
SUBORDER:
Fungiina
FAMILY:
Agariciidae

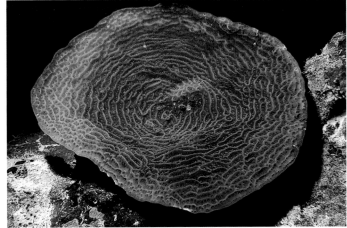

SIZE: Colony 4 - 6 in.
DEPTH: 20 - 180 ft.

Fragile Saucer Coral
Yellow-brown variety.

Fragile Saucer Coral
Constricted leaf coral form contracta; *note pinched corallites.*

(USNM 91646)

137

Leaf, Plate & Sheet Corals

VISUAL ID: Colonies grow in massive, thin sheets or flattened plates that often form large whorls and occasionally spirals and bowls. Concentric rows of long rounded ridges and relatively wide valleys run parallel to the colonies' outer edges. Prominent, white star-like polyps in valleys' centers are distinctive of this species. Ridge ends are often tapered, rather than abruptly intersecting other ridges. Pencil-line thin septa, running between the polyp mouths, alternate in height and thickness (observation may require magnifying glass). Colonies' undersides have no polyps and are quite smooth. Yellow-brown to golden-brown and brown, may have greenish, bluish or grayish tints. Fragile.

ABUNDANCE & DISTRIBUTION: Common Caribbean.

HABITAT & BEHAVIOR: Inhabit sloping reef faces and along walls. One of the most abundant corals on deep reefs and walls. Most common between 65-120 feet. Massive overlapping plates often cover large areas.

NOTE: Also commonly known as "Lamarck's Lettuce-Leaf Coral."

Whitestar Sheet Coral
Detail: note distinctive white star-like polyps.

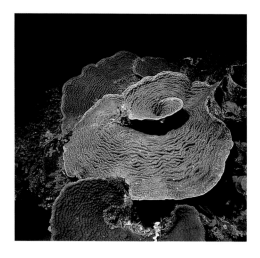

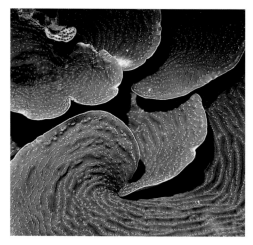

WHITESTAR SHEET CORAL
Agaricia lamarcki
SUBORDER:
Fungiina
FAMILY:
Agariciidae

SIZE: Colony 1 - 6 ft.
DEPTH: 15 - 150 ft.

Whitestar Sheet Coral
Growth patterns.
[left, right & bottom
both pages]

Whitestar Sheet Coral

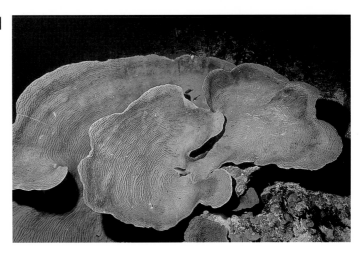

VISUAL ID: Colonies grow rounded, thin blades that commonly curve upward in the shape of fans or bowls often in a spiral design. Concentric rows of long, steep sloped ridges and relatively narrow, V-shaped valleys run parallel to the colonies' pale outer edges. Pale, dimple-like polyps are centered in the valleys. Pencil-line thin septa running between polyp mouths are of equal size (observation may require magnifying glass). Colonies' undersides have no polyps and are quite smooth. Yellow-brown to golden-brown to brown, may have bluish, greenish or grayish tints. Fragile.

ABUNDANCE & DISTRIBUTION: Occasional Caribbean.

HABITAT & BEHAVIOR: Inhabit sloping reef faces and along walls. Most common between 75-150 feet.

NOTE: Also known as "Graham's Lettuce-leaf Coral" and "Graham's Sheet Coral."

Dimpled Sheet Coral
Bowl shaped colonies.

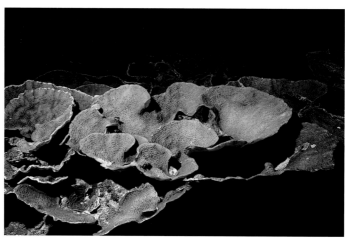

VISUAL ID: Colonies form rounded, thin blades that curve upward on flat or sloping substrate, growing in the shape of fans or bowls. On vertical walls large, spiral curving, overlapping plates may contour to the substrate. Occasionally grow in shingle-like fashion. Running around the upper surface are more-or-less continuous, wide, wavy valleys and ridges that parallel the outer edges. Corallite centers are distinctively nestled in rows against ridges' steep outer edges. Inner ridge faces slope more gently toward colonies' centers. The blades' undersides have no polyps and are quite smooth. Shades of brown to gray, often with yellowish, greenish or bluish tints; outer edge of blades often white. Fragile.

ABUNDANCE & DISTRIBUTION: Occasional Caribbean. Not reported Florida or Bahamas.

HABITAT & BEHAVIOR: Inhabit deep reefs, often on ledges or at the base of deep walls. Most common between 90-150 feet. Massive overlapping colonies occasionally cover large areas of the bottom.

DIMPLED SHEET CORAL
Agaricia grahamae
SUBORDER:
Fungiina
FAMILY:
Agariciidae

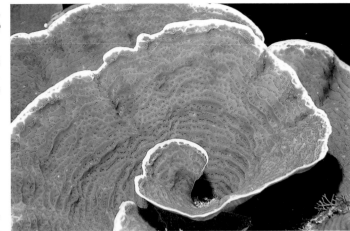

SIZE: Colony 1 - 6 ft.
DEPTH: 50 - 240 ft.

Dimpled Sheet Coral
Detail comparison: Whitestar Sheet Coral (left); note white star-like polyps and rounded ridges; Dimpled Sheet Coral (right); note long parallel valleys with steep sloped ridges.

SCROLL CORAL
Agaricia undata
SUBORDER:
Fungiina
FAMILY:
Agariciidae

SIZE: Colony 1 - 6 ft.
DEPTH: 50 - 250 ft.

continued next page 141

VISUAL IDENTIFICATION KEY
TO SIMILAR APPEARING PLATE & SHEET CORALS

Colonies of the following species often form structures with virtually identical shapes and sizes and often grow mixed together overlapping one another. Distinguishing the different species requires close observation of the valley and ridge structures, polyp placement and septa detail. The following guide should be helpful.

NO RIDGES OR VALLEYS

BOULDER STAR CORAL, *Montastraea annularis,* morphotype (4) [pg. 113]: small, prominently protruding, volcano-like corallites.

HONEYCOMB PLATE CORAL, *Porites colonensis,* [pg. 135]: porous, honeycomb-like corallites.

RIDGES AND VALLEYS, CORALLITES CENTERED IN VALLEYS

WHITESTAR SHEET CORAL, *Agaricia lamarcki,* [pg. 139]: thin, often whorled, plates. Prominent white, star-like polyps distinguish this species.

DIMPLED SHEET CORAL, *Agaricia grahamae,* [pg. 141]: thin, usually upturned plates forming fans and bowls with pale edges. Ridges rise sharply from V-shaped valleys holding dimple-like corallites.

PURPLE LETTUCE CORAL, *Agaricia agaricites* form *purpurea,* [pg. 145]: thick flat plates. Long parallel ridges and valleys mix with numerous short valleys and intersecting ridges. Ridges relatively tall and sharply raised.

RIDGES AND VALLEYS, CORALLITES NESTLED AGAINST RIDGES' OUTER EDGE

SCROLL CORAL, *Agaricia undata,* [pg. 141]: ridges are long and continuous.

SUNRAY LETTUCE CORAL, *Helioseris cucullata,* [pg. 135]: ridges tend to be short and discontinuous, septa more prominent than Scroll Coral [previous].

Scroll Coral
continued from previous page

Colony with large overlapping plates.

Detail: note corallites nestled against ridges' outer edge. [far left]

Shingle-like colonies. [left]

Mixture of colonies including: Lettuce, Scroll and Whitestar Sheet Corals.

Mixture of colonies including: Lettuce, Sunray Lettuce, Whitestar Sheet and Boulder Star Corals.

Leaf, Plate & Sheet Corals

VISUAL ID: Colonies grow in several forms. Form *agaricites* is thickly encrusting or hemispherical with ridges of different heights and discontinuous valleys in reticulated pattern. Form *carinata* grows in thick, flattened plates with prominent ridges and long valleys. Thick, bifacial, low, upright plates or ribbons extend from the surface. Form *purpurea* grows in thick, flat plates and is distinguished by long continuous, parallel valleys with prominent ridges. Colonies may grow in shingle-like fashion. Form *danai* grows a series of overlapping large, thick, bifacial, upright lobes. Tan to yellow-brown, grayish brown, brown and chocolate, can have bluish or purplish tints. Not especially fragile.

ABUNDANCE & DISTRIBUTION: Abundant to common Florida, Bahamas, Caribbean.

HABITAT & BEHAVIOR: Inhabit most marine environments from mangrove and back reef areas to outer reefs and walls. Form *agaricites* is the most common and generally inhabits shallow patch and back reef areas. The other forms are more common on fore reef slopes.

Keeled Lettuce Coral
Form carinata *grows in thick plates with thick, bifacial, upright extensions.*

Purple Lettuce Coral
Form purpurea *grows in flat plates with long continuous, parallel valleys and tall ridges.*

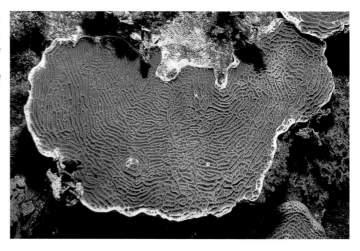

LETTUCE CORAL
Agaricia agaricites
SUBORDER:
Fungiina
FAMILY:
Agariciidae

SIZE: Colony 4 in. - 3 ft.
DEPTH: 3 - 240 ft.

Lettuce Coral
Form agaricites *encrusts with discontinuous valleys and ridges in reticulated patterns.*

Scaled Lettuce Coral
Form danai *grows in series of thick, bifacial, upright lobes.*

VISUAL ID: Colonies form small, generally circular, lumpy encrustations of densely packed corallites in reticulated patterns. Corallites have deep, often narrow or pinched pits. Long valleys or two-faced lobes are never present. Yellow-brown to brown or chocolate; frequently with white areas and blotches where zooxanthellae are absent.

ABUNDANCE & DISTRIBUTION: Occasional South Florida, Bahamas, Caribbean.

HABITAT & BEHAVIOR: Inhabit sloping reefs, undercut faces and canyon walls. Often in somewhat protected locations. Most common between 15-35 feet.

NOTE: This species is regarded by many scientists as a form of Lettuce Coral, *A. agaricites* form *humilis* [previous]. Pictured specimen collected (USNM 91654) and visual identification confirmed by magnified examination.

VISUAL ID: Colonies form low clumps that resemble patches of leaf lettuce. The thin, upright blades have polyps on both sides. Wavy, parallel ridges run horizontally across the blade faces. Shades of brown to gray, often with yellowish, greenish or bluish tints. Blades fairly fragile.

ABUNDANCE & DISTRIBUTION: Abundant Northwest Caribbean, especially along Central American Coast; occasional to absent balance of Caribbean and Bahamas. Not reported Florida.

HABITAT & BEHAVIOR: Inhabit shallow reef tops, especially where wave action produces regular water movement. Numerous adjoining colonies can cover huge areas of reef tops. Most common between 15-30 feet. Narrow areas between blades provide shelter for numerous animals, including brittlestars, sea urchins and small eels. Watercress Alga [pg. 205] often grows between the blades.

Thin Leaf Lettuce Coral

Large colonies may cover huge areas.

LOW RELIEF LETTUCE CORAL
Agaricia humilis
SUBORDER:
Fungiina
FAMILY:
Agariciidae

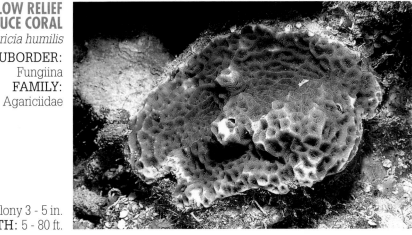

SIZE: Colony 3 - 5 in.
DEPTH: 5 - 80 ft.

THIN LEAF LETTUCE CORAL
Agaricia tenuifolia
SUBORDER:
Fungiina
FAMILY:
Agariciidae

SIZE: Colony 3 - 12 ft.
DEPTH: 6 - 90 ft.

Thin Leaf Lettuce Coral
*Blade detail
of small colony.*

Fleshy Corals

VISUAL ID: Colonies form flat plates, mounds and hemispherical domes with a peripheral ridge that frequently grows inward; there may also be independent ridges. Ridge patterns and the height and depth of valleys vary according to local environmental conditions. Ridges and valleys usually of contrasting colors or shades. Color variable, commonly in shades of green, brown or gray. Colonies and especially ridges may appear fleshy. Tentacles extend only from ridges.

ABUNDANCE & DISTRIBUTION: Occasional South Florida, Bahamas, Caribbean.

HABITAT & BEHAVIOR: Tend to inhabit shaded areas of shallow to moderately deep reefs, more frequently grow in the open with increasing depth. Most common between 25-75 feet deep. Polyps retracted during day.

NOTE: Colonies without formed ridges in the colonies' center were previously classified as a separate species, Lowridge Cactus Coral, *M. daniana*. Many scientists believe these are only young colonies that have not yet formed independent ridges or simply a growth form and should be classified as a single species.

Ridged Cactus Coral
Colonies without central independent ridges were formerly classified as a separate species Lowridge Cactus Coral, M. daniana.

Ridged Cactus Coral
Tentacles partially extended at night along edge of ridges.

RIDGED CACTUS CORAL
Mycetophyllia lamarckiana
SUBORDER:
Faviina
FAMILY:
Mussidae

SIZE: Colony 4 - 15 in.
DEPTH: 10 - 190 ft.

Ridged Cactus Coral
Hemispherical dome growth pattern.

Ridged Cactus Coral
Dying colony showing skeleton.

VISUAL ID: Colonies thickly encrust the bottom and have overhanging edges when the substrate falls away. A robust ridge bordering the colony frequently grows inward; short independent central ridges are also common. In deeper water the central ridges become less pronounced and occasionally disappear. Large, knob-like polyp mouths in the valleys. (Similar appearing Rough Cactus Coral, *M. ferox*, [next] distinguished by small, knob-like polyp mouths and less pronounced ridges.) Ridges and polyp mouths are often of light color contrasting with darker valleys in shades of green, brown, reddish or gray. Tentacles extend only from ridges.

ABUNDANCE & DISTRIBUTION: Occasional South Florida, Bahamas, Caribbean.

HABITAT & BEHAVIOR: Inhabit most moderate to deep reef environments, from patch reefs to steep slopes and wall drop-offs. Most common between 40-130 feet. Polyps retracted during the day.

NOTE: Also commonly known as "Thin Fungus Coral."

Knobby Cactus Coral
Deep water growth pattern without central ridges.

VISUAL ID: Colonies thickly encrust the bottom and have overhanging edges when the substrate falls away. A ridge bordering the colony frequently grows inward crisscrossing the surface often forming closed valleys and giving the colony a lattice-like appearance. In the valleys are small, knob-like polyp mouths. (Similar appearing Ridged Cactus Coral, *M. aliciae*, [previous] distinguished by large, knob-like polyp mouths and more robust ridges.) Ridges and polyp mouths are often of light color contrasting with darker valleys in shades of brown, pink, green, gray and bluish gray. Tentacles extend only from ridges.

ABUNDANCE & DISTRIBUTION: Occasional South Florida, Bahamas, Caribbean.

HABITAT & BEHAVIOR: Tend to inhabit open areas of shallow to mid-range reefs where water flow is very strong. Most common between 30-70 feet. Polyps may be partially extended during the day.

NOTE: Also commonly known as "Grooved Fungus Coral."

KNOBBY CACTUS CORAL
Mycetophyllia aliciae
SUBORDER:
Faviina
FAMILY:
Mussidae

SIZE: Colony 6 - 18 in.
DEPTH: 50 - 240 ft.

Knobby Cactus Coral
Young colony;
note large, knob-like
polyp mouths
in valleys.

**ROUGH
CACTUS CORAL**
Mycetophyllia ferox
SUBORDER:
Faviina
FAMILY:
Mussidae

SIZE: Colony 1 - 2 ft.
DEPTH: 2 - 120 ft.

continued next page 151

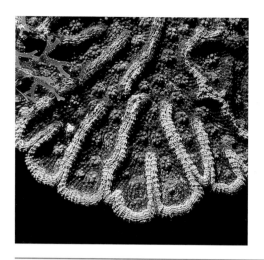

VISUAL ID: Colonies thinly encrust, usually as circular plates, that generally conform to the contours of the substrate. Only member of the genus without central ridges. Surface covered with smooth, rounded bumps (polyp mouths). (Similar appearing deep colonies of Great Star Coral, *Montastraea cavernosa*, [pg. 115] are distinguished by well-defined corallites.) Shades of marbled green, brown, gray, blue-gray and may have iridescent tints. Colonies do not have tentacles.

ABUNDANCE & DISTRIBUTION: Occasional Bahamas, Caribbean. Not reported Florida.

HABITAT & BEHAVIOR: Inhabit shaded areas of deep reefs; most common along walls.

Ridgeless Cactus Coral
Color variety.

Rough Cactus Coral
continued from previous page

Colony encrusting reef top.

Detail: note knob-like polyp mouths. [far left]

Green variation. [left]

RIDGELESS CACTUS CORAL
Mycetophyllia reesi

SUBORDER: Faviina

FAMILY: Mussidae

SIZE: Colony 1 - 2 ft.
DEPTH: 60 - 220 ft.

Ridgeless Cactus Coral
Color variation.

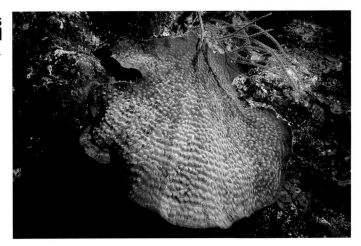

VISUAL ID: Colonies form small, oval to hemispherical domes. Highly convoluted with fleshy ridges and deep, narrow valleys. (Small colonies of similar Ridged Cactus Coral [pg.149] distinguished by wider valleys and less prominent ridges.) Colors quite variable, including shades of yellow, green, brown and gray. Occasionally iridescent tints of orange or blue. Ridges and valleys usually of contrasting shades or colors. Light colored, thin line along ridge tops.

ABUNDANCE & DISTRIBUTION: Populations highly variable from locality to locality; abundant to rare South Florida, Bahamas, Caribbean.

HABITAT & BEHAVIOR: Inhabit a wide range of shallow water environments, including fringing reefs, back reefs, patch reefs and areas of high sedimentation. Most common between 3-30 feet. Polyps retracted during day.

NOTE: Common name comes from sharp skeletal spines which are hidden under the fleshy tissue. Also commonly known as "Cactus Coral," "Fleshy Cactus Coral" and "Stalked Cactus Coral."

Rough Star Coral
Gray color variety.

VISUAL ID: Colonies form small oval to hemispherical domes. Fleshy ridges with rough, irregular closed polygonal valleys. Valleys usually contain only one or two polyps. Light colored, thin line along ridge tops. Ridges commonly brown or gray, occasionally green, pinkish or even purple; valleys pale to white.

ABUNDANCE & DISTRIBUTION: Common to occasional South Florida, Bahamas, Florida.

HABITAT & BEHAVIOR: Inhabit a wide range of shallow water environments, including fringing reefs, back reefs, patch reefs and areas of high sedimentation. Most common between 10-35 feet. Polyps retracted during day.

NOTE: Also commonly known as "Polygonal Coral."

SINUOUS CACTUS CORAL
Isophyllia sinuosa
SUBORDER:
Faviina
FAMILY:
Mussidae

SIZE: Colony 2 ½ - 8 in.
DEPTH: 3 - 85 ft.

Sinuous Cactus Coral
*Pale color variation
with dark stripe
on ridge tops.*

ROUGH STAR CORAL
Isophyllastrea rigida
SUBORDER:
Faviina
FAMILY:
Mussidae

SIZE: Colony 3 - 7 in.
DEPTH: 3 - 65 ft.

VISUAL ID: Single, large, fleshy, circular to oval polyp. Underlying skeleton often evident in the form of raised radiating lines. Central area of corallite usually flat to somewhat convex, rarely concave. Darker shades of gray to brown, green, and blue-green; base color often radially streaked with lighter shade. May fluoresce. Positive identification of this and the next two species requires magnified examination (see next description). There are no visual clues distinguishing Solitary Disk Coral [next]; Atlantic Mushroom Coral [next page] usually has a rougher texture and lighter colors.

ABUNDANCE & DISTRIBUTION: Occasional South Florida, Bahamas, Caribbean.

HABITAT & BEHAVIOR: Generally inhabit deep reefs and walls, occasionally shallower. Prefer shaded areas on rocky substrates and also grow in low-light conditions under ledge overhangs and in cave openings. Polyp tentacles retracted during day.

NOTE: Visual identification of pictured specimens was verified by collection and magnified examination of septa. Also commonly known as "Solitary Disk Coral" and "Smooth Disk Coral."

Artichoke Coral
Juveniles, such as pictured specimen, cannot be positively identified.

VISUAL ID: Single, large, fleshy, circular to oval polyp. Underlying skeleton often evident in the form of raised radiating lines. Central area of corallite usually flat to somewhat concave, rarely convex. Darker shades of gray to brown, green, and blue-green; base color often radially streaked with lighter shade. May fluoresce. Smallest of the three disk coral species. Positive identification requires magnified examination of erect projections growing from the septa, called teeth. This species has rough, irregular, thin, cylindrical teeth; Artichoke Coral [previous] has spike or pick-shaped teeth; and Atlantic Mushroom [next] has large, triangular teeth.

ABUNDANCE & DISTRIBUTION: Occasional South Florida, Bahamas, Caribbean.

HABITAT & BEHAVIOR: Generally inhabit deep reefs and walls, occasionally shallower. Prefer shaded areas on rocky substrates and also grow in low-light conditions under ledge overhangs and in cave openings. Polyp tentacles retracted during day.

NOTE: Visual identification of pictured specimens was verified by collection (USNM 91560) and magnified examination of septa.

ARTICHOKE CORAL
Scolymia cubensis
SUBORDER:
Faviina
FAMILY:
Mussidae

SIZE: Polyp 1 ½ - 4 in.
DEPTH: 30 - 260 ft.

Artichoke Coral
Color variation.

(USNM 91664)

SOLITARY DISK CORAL
Scolymia wellsi
SUBORDER:
Faviina
FAMILY:
Mussidae

SIZE: Polyp 1 - 2 ¾ in.
DEPTH: 30 - 260 ft.

continued next page **157**

Solitary Disk Coral
Color variation.

(USNM 91665)

VISUAL ID: Single, large, fleshy, circular to oval polyp with rough, warty texture. Central area of corallite usually concave to flat, rarely convex. Lighter shades of gray to green, blue-green and brown. (Generally texture rougher and color shades lighter than two previous species.) Caribbean's largest solitary polyp coral. Size alone can confirm identification if over four inches. If less, positive identification requires magnified examination of corallite structure (see previous description).

ABUNDANCE & DISTRIBUTION: Occasional South Florida, Bahamas, Caribbean.

HABITAT & BEHAVIOR: Inhabit deep reef environments and walls. Most common between 60-100 feet. Prefer well-lighted areas on rocky substrates and outcroppings. Polyp tentacles normally retracted during day, but be extended in turbid conditions.

NOTE: Visual identification of pictured specimens was verified by magnified examination of triangular septal teeth. D.P. Fenner concludes that this is not a separate species, but a form of Spiny Flower Coral [next], *Bull. Mar. Sci.,* Vol. 53, No.3, 1993.

Solitary Disk Coral
continued from previous page

Color variation.

(USNM 91661)

ATLANTIC MUSHROOM CORAL
Scolymia lacera

SUBORDER:
Faviina
FAMILY:
Mussidae

SIZE: Polyp 2¹/₂ - 6 in.
DEPTH: 30 - 260 ft.

Atlantic Mushroom Coral
Color varieties.

VISUAL ID: Colonies formed of large fleshy polyps with rough, blemished texture. Although the polyps are well-separated on the tips of a branched structure, their expanded fleshy tissues press against adjacent individuals so tightly that an overall colony appears as a solid mound. The polyp's skeleton, composed of numerous sharp spiked plates (septa) [below right], is the source of the common name. Shades of gray, may have tints of green, blue and even fluorescent reddish orange or pink (fluorescent color disappears if hand light or strobe is used).

ABUNDANCE & DISTRIBUTION: Common to occasional South Florida, Bahamas, Caribbean.

HABITAT & BEHAVIOR: Inhabit most reef environments, will also tolerate turbit environments. Most common between 20-80 feet. Polyps extend tentacles at night.

NOTE: Also commonly known as "Large Flower Coral."

VISUAL ID: Colonial polyps, often in small clusters. Corallites cone-shaped with circular to elliptical rims and deep central pits. Tall, thin, rounded, protruding septa radiate from the pit and extend around the rim lip. Often lavender or white, occasionally pink or pale green. Fragile. Ahermatypic and azooxanthellate.

ABUNDANCE & DISTRIBUTION: Occasional Caribbean. Not reported Florida or Bahamas.

HABITAT & BEHAVIOR: Inhabit the ceilings of caves, under ledge overhangs, usually where there is some water circulation. Most common below 80 feet.

NOTE: Visual identification of pictured specimens confirmed by collection (USNM 92084) and magnified examination.

SPINY FLOWER CORAL
Mussa angulosa
SUBORDER:
Faviina
FAMILY:
Mussidae

SIZE: Colony ½ - 2 ft.
Polyp 1 ½ - 4 in.
DEPTH: 5 - 180 ft.

Spiny Flower Coral
Green color variation.

*Polyp tentacles
partially extended at night.*
[far left]

*Comparison of living
and dead polyps: note
triangular septal teeth.*
[left]

BAROQUE CAVE CORAL
Thalamophyllia riisei
SUBORDER:
Caryophylliina
FAMILY:
Caryophylliidae

SIZE: Polyp ¼ - ½ in.
DEPTH: 50 - 1,000 ft.

VISUAL ID: Clumps of widely spaced polyps on long stalks, that appear to originate from a central core, form hemispherical mounds. Corallites round to oval. Shades of yellow-brown to brown and gray, often with blue to blue-green to green tinting that may be somewhat iridescent. A rare variant, form *flabellata*, is distinguished by extremely long (up to six inches), narrow (about one-half inch) corallites.

ABUNDANCE & DISTRIBUTION: Common to occasional Florida, Bahamas, Caribbean; also north to North Carolina.

HABITAT & BEHAVIOR: Inhabit most reef environments, prefer somewhat shaded, protected areas. Most common between 15-90 feet. Occasionally multiple colonies cover large area of the reef. Extend tentacles at night.

**Smooth
Flower Coral**
Extended polyp detail.

**Smooth
Flower Coral**
*Corallite detail,
typical form.*

SMOOTH FLOWER CORAL
Eusmilia fastigiata
SUBORDER:
Caryophylliina
FAMILY:
Caryophylliidae

SIZE: Colony $1/2$ - $2\,1/2$ ft.
Polyps $3/4$ - $1\,1/4$ in.
DEPTH: 3 - 200 ft.

Smooth Flower Coral
Colony with polyps extended at night.

Smooth Flower Coral
Elongate Smooth Flower Coral form flabellata, *corallite detail.*

Cup & Flower Corals

VISUAL ID: Brilliant red to orange or yellow polyp clumps that often form hemispherical mounds. Tissue covering skeleton usually deeper red to orange, while tentacles often bright orange to yellow. Colonies may contain only a few or hundreds of polyps. Ahermatypic and azooxanthellate.

ABUNDANCE & DISTRIBUTION: Scattered distribution throughout Bahamas, eastern and southern Caribbean. May be abundant in localized areas, while absent in similar environments around same island. Absent or rare northwest Caribbean, Florida and Gulf of Mexico. Also Indo-Pacific.

HABITAT & BEHAVIOR: Prefer shaded areas in a wide range of environments, from pilings under docks, to caves in shallow reefs, to undercut faces and walls on deeper reefs. A clear water species that prefers some water movement. A few polyps may be extended during day, but full extension of entire colony normally occurs only at night.

NOTE: Orange Cup Coral is believed to be the only species of stony coral introduced to the western Atlantic. The species was first recorded in 1943 from Puerto Rico and Curacao. Interestingly some specimens collected in the Netherlands Antilles between 1948 and 1950 came from a ship's hull. Since that period the species abundance at these localities has been increasing. Orange Cup Coral has also been observed at numerous additional sites. If sighting dates and locations are plotted on a map it is easy to theorize that the species was transported into the Caribbean on a ship's bottom from either the eastern Pacific or tropical Indo-Pacific, where the opportunistic species is common, and has dispersed by following typical current patterns throughout the region. (Stephen D. Cairns, *Revision of the Shallow-Water Azooxanthellate Scleractinia of the Western Atlantic, Studies of the Natural History of the Caribbean Region,* 2000, Vol. 75)

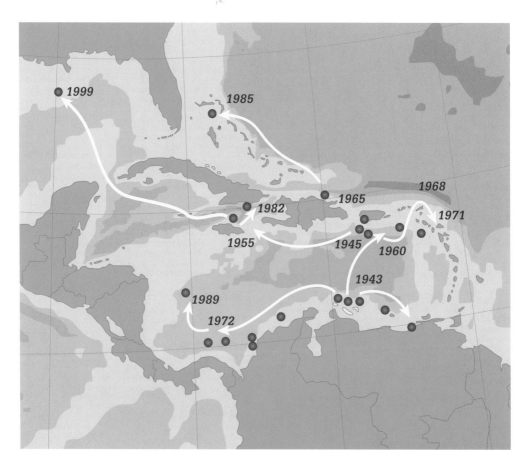

ORANGE CUP CORAL
Tubastraea coccinea

SUBORDER:
Dendrophylliina
FAMILY:
Dendrophylliidae

SIZE: Colony 3 - 12 in.
Polyp ½ - ¾ in.
DEPTH: 3 - 120 ft.

Orange Cup Coral
Hemispherical colony.

*Colonies on
undercut reef face.*
[below left]

*Colonies on
dock piling at night.*
[below right]

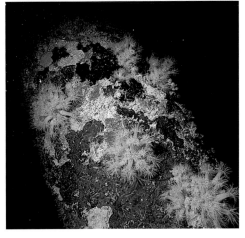

VISUAL ID: Small, solitary polyp. Corallite cone-shaped with base re-expanding to encrust and attach to hard substrate (occasionally free when base attaches to and envelopes a small pebble). Rim (calice) of corallite oval to elliptical. Twelve large septa of equal size can be seen by unaided eye, with several smaller septa between. Small septal ridges continue down sides of corallite resulting in a corrugated texture. Red to pink, orange, light brown and white. Ahermatypic and azooxanthellate.

ABUNDANCE & DISTRIBUTION: Uncommon (within safe diving limits) Florida, Bahamas, Caribbean.

HABITAT & BEHAVIOR: Inhabit areas with hard substrates or gravel. Bases may be covered with sand or gravel exposing only the rims of corallites. Tend to inhabit shallower waters off Florida's northern coasts.

NOTE: Pictured specimen collected (USNM 92271) at 80 feet, off Jacksonville, Florida; identification confirmed by magnified examination.

VISUAL ID: Colonial; corallites may be clustered in small groups or appear to be solitary. Solitary examples are joined to nearby corallites by encrusting bases that may be hidden from view by overgrowing organisms. Corallites are slightly tapering and cylindrical with flared rims (calice). Six, tall, thick primary septa, and six smaller secondary septa can be seen by unaided eye. Fine septal ridges continue down sides of corallites resulting in a subtle corrugated texture, although not always obvious to the unaided eye. Bright orange to pink. Ahermatypic and azooxanthellate.

ABUNDANCE & DISTRIBUTION: Occasional Caribbean, Bahamas and Gulf of Mexico.

HABITAT & BEHAVIOR: Inhabit dark recesses such as cave ceilings and under ledge overhangs.

NOTE: Identification of pictured specimens confirmed by collection and magnified examination: right (USNM 91651) at 15 feet, Roatan, Honduras; below (USNM 91655) at 65 ft, Conception Island, Bahamas; below right (USNM 91659) at 85 feet, San Salvador, Bahamas.

**Orange
Solitary Coral**
*Note corrugated texture
of corallite's sides.*

POROUS CUP CORAL
Balanophyllia floridana
SUBORDER:
Dendrophylliina
FAMILY:
Dendrophylliidae

SIZE: Diameter ¹/₂ - 1 in.
Height ³/₄ - 1 ¹/₂ in.
DEPTH: 80 - 600 ft.

ORANGE SOLITARY CORAL
Rhizopsammia goesi
SUBORDER:
Dendrophylliina
FAMILY:
Dendrophylliidae

SIZE: Diameter ¹/₄ - ¹/₂ in.
Height ¹/₄ - ¹/₂ in.
DEPTH: 15-385 ft.

Orange Solitary Coral
Solitary appearing corallites are joined by encrusting bases.

Cup & Flower Corals

VISUAL ID: Colonies form a thin encrusting base from which corallites protrude. Often the corallites appear unconnected because of overgrowing sponge, algae and other organisms, but the connection between two or three individuals is usually obvious. Corallites are circular to elliptical with tall, thin, rounded, protruding septa around the rims and deep central pits. There are usually twelve obvious, large septa of nearly equal size, and numerous smaller ones depending on corallite size. (Similar Lesser Speckled Cup Coral [next] has only six large septa.) Orange-brown, brown, pink and lavender; central pit often pale green. Brown speckled pigmentation is distinctive of this species. Occasionally large individual polyps do not show this pigmentation. Ahermatypic and azooxanthellate.

ABUNDANCE & DISTRIBUTION: Common Caribbean; occasional Florida, Bahamas.

HABITAT & BEHAVIOR: Inhabit the ceilings of caves, under ledge overhangs, and occasionally on the underside of deep sheet and plate corals.

(USNM 91652)

(USNM 92081)

VISUAL ID: Colonies form small encrusting groups of polyps. Often the corallites appear unconnected because of overgrowing sponge, algae and other organisms. Corallites are circular to elliptical with deep central pits. Six tall, thin, rounded septa protrude noticeably around the rim. (Similar Speckled Cup Coral [previous] distinguished by twelve large septa of nearly equal size.) Numerous smaller septa are usually apparent. Light green, orange-brown, brown, pink, lavender and white. May have some brown speckled pigmentation. Center (mouth area of polyp) often of lighter and/or different color. Ahermatypic and azooxanthellate.

ABUNDANCE & DISTRIBUTION: Occasional Florida, Bahamas, Caribbean.

HABITAT & BEHAVIOR: Attach to and encrust the underside of plate corals, rocks, ledge overhangs and cave ceilings. Often only the top of the polyp is visible because the body is hidden by encrusting sponge, algae or other growths.

NOTE: Pictured specimens collected (USNM 91658) and visual identification confirmed by magnified examination.

SPECKLED CUP CORAL
Rhizosmilia maculata
SUBORDER:
Caryophylliina
FAMILY:
Caryophylliidae

SIZE: Corallite ¹/₄ - ¹/₂ in.,
max. 1 in.
DEPTH: 10 - 500 ft.

Speckled Cup Coral
*Brown variety
with green centers;
note dark brown
speckles.*

Large single polyps.
[left]

LESSER SPECKLED CUP CORAL
Colangia immersa
SUBORDER:
Caryophylliina
FAMILY:
Caryophylliidae

SIZE: Polyp ¹/₂ in.
DEPTH: 10 - 300 ft.

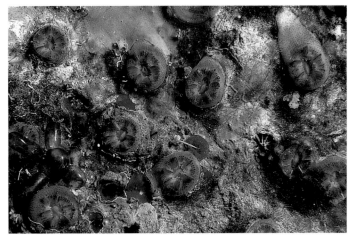

continued next page

Cup & Flower Corals

Lesser Speckled Cup Coral

Lavender variation encrusting underside of a ledge overhang.

(USNM 92091)

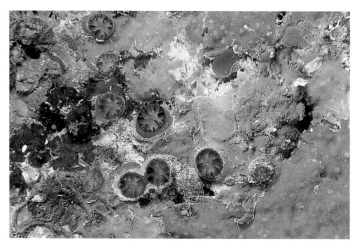

VISUAL ID: Colonies form small encrusting groups of polyps. Often the corallites appear unconnected because of overgrowing sponge, algae and other organisms. Corallites are tall and cylindrical with sharp, prickly protrusions and deep central pits. Six tall, thin, rounded septa and six, somewhat smaller, secondary septa protrude noticeably around the circular rims. Smaller septa are usually apparent. White to brown with speckles. Ahermatypic and azooxanthellate.

ABUNDANCE & DISTRIBUTION: Rare Caribbean.

HABITAT & BEHAVIOR: Inhabit dark, deep recesses of cave ceilings. Other habitats unknown (see note). Often only the top of the polyp is visible because the body is hidden by encrusting sponge, algae or other growths.

NOTE: Pictured specimen collected at 35 feet, off Isla Cayos Cochinos, Honduras. Identification confirmed by magnified examination of corallites. (USMN 99247)

VISUAL ID: Colonies form small encrusting groups of polyps. Corallites circular with deep central pits. Six protruding primary and six, somewhat smaller, secondary septa around rims. Brown color, ranging from yellow-brown to brown to red-brown is distinctive of this species. Never speckled like similar Speckled Cup Coral [previous page]. Ahermatypic and azooxanthellate.

ABUNDANCE & DISTRIBUTION: Occasional Florida, Bahamas, Caribbean.

HABITAT & BEHAVIOR: Attach to and encrust the underside of rocks, ledge overhangs and cave ceilings. Often only the top of the polyp is visible because the body is hidden by encrusting sponge, algae or other growths. Most common between 1-60 feet.

NOTE: There are two subspecies: *P. americana americana* in the western Atlantic, *P. americana mouchezii* occurs in the eastern Atlantic.

Lesser Speckled Cup Coral

continued from previous page

Encrusting ceiling of a shallow tidal cave.

(USNM 92086)

CRYPTIC CAVE CORAL
Colangia jamaicaensis
SUBORDER:
Caryophylliina
FAMILY:
Caryophylliidae

SIZE: Polyp ¹/₄ in.
DEPTH: 35 ft. (see note)

HIDDEN CUP CORAL
Phyllangia americana americana
SUBORDER:
Caryophylliina
FAMILY:
Caryophylliidae

SIZE: Polyp ¹/₂ in.
DEPTH: 1 - 100 ft.

continued next page **171**

Hidden Cup Coral
Colony on ceiling of shipwreck.

VISUAL ID: Colonies appear as scattered groups of tiny individual polyps; however, corallite bases are joined by thin, often obscured encrustations. Corallites cylindrical; septa often appear as rows of whitish dots radiating from centers and wrapping around rims. Shades of red-brown to brown. Ahermatypic and azooxanthellate.

ABUNDANCE & DISTRIBUTION: Occasional Florida, Bahamas, Caribbean.

HABITAT & BEHAVIOR: Attach to and encrust the underside of rocks, coral rubble, ledge overhangs and cave ceilings. Often only the tip of the polyp is visible because the body is hidden by encrusting sponge, algae or other growths. Most common between 1-20 feet.

NOTE: Visual identification of pictured specimens confirmed by collection (USNM 92090) and magnified examination.

Dwarf Cup Coral
Encrusting wall of cave.

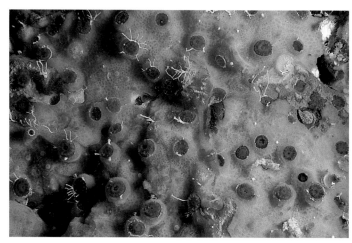

(USNM 91656)

Hidden Cup Coral
continued from previous page

Yellow-brown variation.

(USNM 92086)

DWARF CUP CORAL
Astrangia solitaria
SUBORDER:
Faviina
FAMILY:
Rhizangiidae

SIZE: Polyp diameter
$^1/_8$ - $^1/_4$ in.
height $^1/_8$ - $^3/_4$ in.
DEPTH: 1 - 135 ft.

Dwarf Cup Coral
Polyps extended.

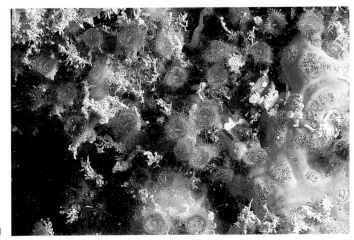

(USNM 91657)

173

VISUAL ID: Colonies form clusters of circular to oval corallites with common encrusting base. Numerous, tall rounded septa and separated inner ends (pali) in central pit visible to unaided eye. Colonies expand by asexual budding from the edges of common base. Septa red-brown; pali and central pit white. Ahermatypic and azooxanthellate.

ABUNDANCE & DISTRIBUTION: Uncommon Bahamas, Caribbean, Gulf of Mexico.

HABITAT & BEHAVIOR: Attach to and encrust the underside ledge overhangs and cave ceilings.

NOTE: Pictured specimen collected (USNM 92280) at 125 feet, off West Caicos, Turks & Caicos Islands and visual identification confirmed by magnified examination.

VISUAL ID: Colonies formed of circular corallites with common encrusting base. Six to twelve high rounded septa, with several smaller septa between and numerous lobes in central pit visible to unaided eye. Colonies expand by asexual budding from the edges of common base. Shades of white, occasionally tinted with pink. Ahermatypic and azooxanthellate.

ABUNDANCE & DISTRIBUTION: Rare off West Palm Beach. Additional distribution unknown (See note).

HABITAT & BEHAVIOR: Attach to and encrust the underside ledge overhangs and cave ceilings.

NOTE: Formerly an undescribed species discovered by Paul Humann at 70 feet off Palm Beach, FL. and named in his honor. (USNM 92080)

VISUAL ID: Solitary, cylindrical, circular to slightly elliptical corallites with twelve large, rounded septa, and three smaller septa between visible to unaided eye. Separated inner ends of septa (pali) form a light colored elliptical ring around deep central pit. Upper half of corallite shades of brown; basal deposits creamy white. Ahermatypic and azooxanthellate.

ABUNDANCE & DISTRIBUTION: Uncommon Bahamas, Caribbean. Not reported Florida.

HABITAT & BEHAVIOR: Firmly attach to hard substrate on the underside of ledge overhangs and cave ceilings. Occasionally in the recesses of small cavities.

NOTE: Pictured specimen collected (USNM 91667) at 70 feet, off San Salvador, Bahamas; visual identification confirmed by magnified examination.

TWOTONE CUP CORAL
Phacelocyathus flos
SUBORDER:
Caryophylliina
FAMILY:
Caryophylliidae

SIZE: Polyp diameter
$^{1}/_{4}$ - $^{1}/_{2}$ in.
DEPTH: 70 - 1,700 ft.

ORNATE CUP CORAL
Coenocyathus humanni
SUBORDER:
Caryophylliida
FAMILY:
Caryophylliidae

SIZE: Polyp diameter
$^{1}/_{8}$ - $^{1}/_{4}$ in.
DEPTH: 70 ft. (see note)

BUTTON CUP CORAL
Coenocyathus caribbeana
SUBORDER:
Caryophylliida
FAMILY:
Caryophylliidae

SIZE: Polyp diameter
$^{1}/_{8}$ - $^{1}/_{4}$ in.
DEPTH: 50 - 550 ft.

Class Anthozoa
Order Antipatharia

(An-tih-path-AIR-ee-ah / Gr. against disease)

Black Corals

Black corals are generally thought to be deep dwellers, but about half of the approximately 30 species in the Caribbean area can be found within safe scuba diving depths and several grow in surprisingly shallow water. Black coral polyps secrete a protein material, usually black in color, that becomes extremely hard and strong by a tanning process. This material is laid down in **concentric layers** forming branched or wire-like structures (skeleton). When a branch is crosscut these layers resemble the growth rings of a tree. The branching pattern of many species is unique and often the key to visual identification. Several species have tiny branchlets called **pinnules.**

Black coral polyps do not form corallite "homes" like stony corals, but instead simply live on the skeletal surface. Each polyp has six, small, non-retractable **tentacles** that can, however, expand or contract to some degree. The tentacles are normally visible to the unaided eye and are an important key in recognizing a colonial structure as black coral. The individual polyps of many species are recognizable because they are spaced apart from one another and their clusters of tentacles resemble barbs of barbed wire. Polyps of other species are spaced close so together that they are difficult to distinguish and appear as a mass of inseparable tentacles.

The polyp tissue of most black corals is somewhat translucent and color pigments only tint the colony gray, brown, rust-red, or green. Occasionally the pigments may be intense and dramatic, especially wire corals which are bright yellow-green or red.

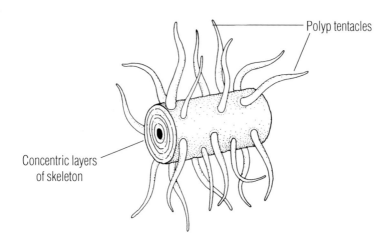

Polyp tentacles

Concentric layers
of skeleton

A few black coral species attain considerable size and their branches are collected, cut, fashioned, polished and sold by jewelers as a semiprecious material. The value of these trinkets comes more from jewelers' propaganda of rareness and the danger associated with deep diving to collect branches, than from any innate property of the material itself. In fact, the black coral species most frequently used by jewelers is neither rare or found particularly deep — on occasion a snorkeler might even sight a colony! Unfortunately, it is now rare in many areas from overharvesting. The great black coral forests of Grand Cayman and Cozumel are only a memory. It will take these slow growing colonies over 100 years to reestablish themselves.

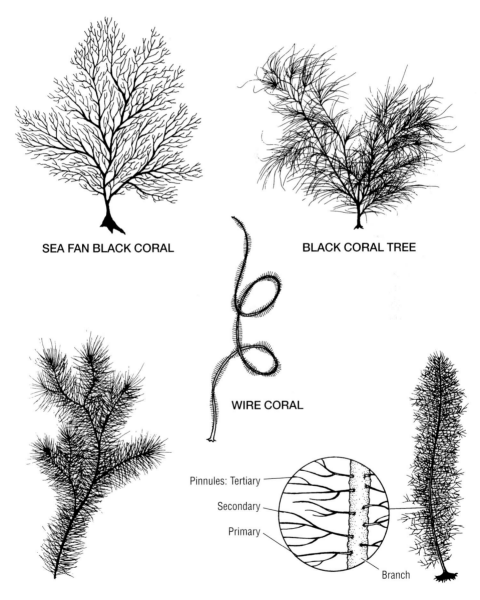

SEA FAN BLACK CORAL

BLACK CORAL TREE

WIRE CORAL

Pinnules: Tertiary

Secondary

Primary

Branch

BOTTLE-BRUSH BUSH BLACK CORAL

BOTTLE BRUSH BLACK CORAL

Black Corals

VISUAL ID: Bushy, branched colonies of primary stalks, with long, thin, scraggly branchlets. Primary branches golden-brown to brown to black and may be tinted red, green or blue. Branchlets are often of lighter color. It is now rare to see colonies over four feet in height because of overharvesting (see note).

ABUNDANCE & DISTRIBUTION: Common to uncommon Bahamas, Caribbean; rare South Florida. Because of overharvesting, now rare in many locations.

HABITAT & BEHAVIOR: In shallow water, occasionally inhabit caves and under large overhangs. In deep water, primarily inhabit canyons and wall faces with some current or periodic water movement. Most common between 80 and 240 feet; in many locations rarely found above 150 feet because of over harvesting.

NOTE: This species, prized by the jewelry industry, is often called "Kings Coral."

SIMILAR SPECIES: *A. salix* often confused with this species is common between 300-1000 feet.

(USNM 92276)

VISUAL ID: Profuse primary and secondary branches extend from a holdfast in nearly a single plane. Thin, pinnate branchlets line either side of the secondary branches, resembling large feathers. Primary and secondary branches golden-brown to brown, gray and black; may be tinted red, green or blue. Branchlets are often of lighter color.

ABUNDANCE & DISTRIBUTION: Common to uncommon Bahamas, Caribbean; rare South Florida.

HABITAT & BEHAVIOR: In shallow water, inhabit caves and under large overhangs. In deep water, inhabit most reef environments including reef slopes, and along walls. Most common between 60 and 180 feet. Often in old deep shipwrecks. A few species of small stalked barnacles [See *Reef Creature Identification*] and other invertebrates often live in association this coral.

NOTE: Formerly classified in the genus *Antipathes*.

BUSHY BLACK CORAL
Antipathes caribbeana
ORDER:
Antipatharia

Bushy Black Coral

Bushy colony.
[far left]

Branch/polyp detail.
[left]

SIZE: 2 - 12 ft.
DEPTH: 40 - 300 ft.

FEATHER BLACK CORAL
Plumapathes pennacea
ORDER:
Antipatharia

SIZE: 1 - 5 ft.
DEPTH: 15 - 1000 ft.

continued next

Black Corals

VISUAL ID: Upright colonies of stiff, coarse, primary and secondary branches extend in nearly a single plane. Occasionally, somewhat bushy. Bright orangish brown to orange-red. (Similar Gray Sea Fan Black Coral [next] distinguished by gray to greenish color, with network of fine, delicate branches.)

ABUNDANCE & DISTRIBUTION: Occasional Bahamas, Caribbean; rare South Florida.

HABITAT & BEHAVIOR: Inhabit most deep environments, often at the base of walls or in the open on reef tops. Prefer areas with good water circulation. Generally inhabit more open areas than similar Gray Sea Fan Black Coral [next].

Orange Sea Fan Black Coral

Sparsely branched colony.

Feather Black Coral

continued from previous page

Branchlet/polyp detail

Grayish variation.
[far left]

Golden brown variation.
[left]

ORANGE SEA FAN BLACK CORAL

Antipathes gracilis

ORDER: Antipatharia

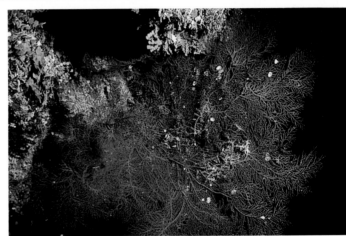

SIZE: 1½ - 4 ft.
DEPTH: 60 - 300 ft.

Orange Sea Fan Black Coral

Unusual thickly branched colony.

Black Corals

VISUAL ID: Colonies shaped like large, classic sea fans with radiating primary branches and a network of numerous, fine, delicate, occasionally interconnecting secondary branches. Polyps shades of pale gray, sometimes tinged with pink, to greenish gray and dark gray; branches black. (Similar Orange Sea Fan Black Coral [previous] distinguished by bright orangish brown to red-brown color, and heavier, coarser, more bushy branches.)

ABUNDANCE & DISTRIBUTION: Occasional Bahamas, Caribbean; rare South Florida.

HABITAT & BEHAVIOR: Inhabit shaded deep reef environments, especially in canyons, crevices, under ledge overhangs and along walls where there is good water circulation. Generally more recluse than similar Orange Sea Fan Black Coral [previous].

Gray Sea Fan Black Coral
Unusually bushy colony.

VISUAL ID: Colonies form highly, subdivided tangled networks of fine branches that contour to the substrate. (Similar Scraggly Black Coral [next] distinguished by thicker, rigid, coarse branches.) Colonies do not protrude more than an inch or so above the substrate. Shades of brown to gray.

ABUNDANCE & DISTRIBUTION: Common Bahamas, Caribbean; occasional to uncommon South Florida.

HABITAT & BEHAVIOR: Inhabit shaded areas under ledge overhangs, cave ceilings and recessed wall faces.

NOTE: Pictured specimen collected (USNM 92277) at 90 feet, off Roatan, Honduras; visual identification confirmed by laboratory examination.

**GRAY SEA FAN
BLACK CORAL**
Antipathes atlantica
ORDER:
Antipatharia

SIZE: 1¹/₂ - 4 ft.
DEPTH: 60 - 300 ft.

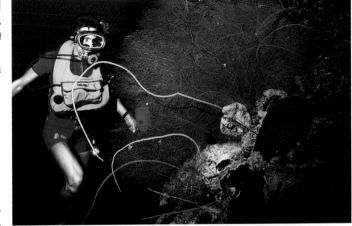

**Gray Sea Fan
Black Coral**
*Note delicate net-like
structure.*

**HAIR NET
BLACK CORAL**
Antipathes lenta
ORDER:
Antipatharia

SIZE: 4 - 10 in.
DEPTH: 80 - 250 ft.

Black Corals

VISUAL ID: Colonies, with a single holdfast, form bramble bush-like tangles of rigid, coarse branches that contour to the substrate. (Similar Hair Net Black Coral [previous] distinguished by finer, more flexible branches.) Colonies do not protrude more than an inch or so above the substrate. Stalk structures gray to black; expanded polyp tentacles pale to translucent.

ABUNDANCE & DISTRIBUTION: Common Caribbean, Bahamas.

HABITAT & BEHAVIOR: Inhabit shaded areas under ledge overhangs, cave ceilings and undercut wall faces.

NOTE: Pictured specimen collected (USNM 92274) at 90 feet, off Roatan, Honduras; visual identification confirmed by laboratory examination.

VISUAL ID: Bushy, upright colonies formed by openly branched primary and secondary stalks. (Similar Scraggly Bottle-brush [next] is more sparsely branched.) Numerous pinnules extend radially from stalks. Primary pinnules both long and short. There are occasional secondary pinnules, but tertiary pinnules are rare. Shades of gray to greenish gray and olive. Young colonies may have only a single, unbranched stalk and require microscopic examination for positive identification.

ABUNDANCE & DISTRIBUTION: Occasional to uncommon Florida, Bahamas, Caribbean.

HABITAT & BEHAVIOR: Inhabit deep reefs and gently sloping drop-offs.

NOTE: Formerly classified in the genus Antipathes.

VISUAL ID: Colonies formed by sparsely branched primary and secondary stalks. (Similar Bottle-brush Bush [previous] is more heavily branched.) Numerous pinnules extend radially from stalks. Primary pinnules long and generally of equal length. There are occasional secondary pinnules, but tertiary pinnules are rare. Shades of gray. Young colonies may have only single, unbranched stalks. (**NOTE:** colony pictured is young and just starting to branch near base.)

ABUNDANCE & DISTRIBUTION: Occasional to uncommon Florida, Bahamas, Caribbean.

HABITAT & BEHAVIOR: Inhabit deep reefs and gently sloping drop-offs; occasionally in old shipwrecks.

NOTE: Positive identification requires microscopic examination. Pictured specimen collected (USNM 92278) at 90 feet, off West Palm Beach, Florida; visual identification confirmed in laboratory. Formerly classified in the genus Antipathes.

184

SCRAGGLY BLACK CORAL
Antipathes umbratica
ORDER:
Antipatharia

SIZE: 6 - 12 in.
DEPTH: 60 - 250 ft.

BOTTLE-BRUSH BUSH BLACK CORAL
Tanacetipathes hirta
ORDER:
Antipatharia

SIZE: 1 - 2¹/₂ ft.
Pinnules 1 - 2 in.
DEPTH: 90 - 200 ft.

SCRAGGLY BOTTLE-BRUSH BLACK CORAL
Tanacetipathes barbadensis
ORDER:
Antipatharia

SIZE: 1 - 2 ft.
Pinnules 2 in.
DEPTH: 90 - 200 ft.

Black Corals

VISUAL ID: Colonies formed by long, unbranched primary stalks, from which numerous pinnules extend radially. Both secondary and tertiary pinnules common, giving the stalks a bushier appearance than Bottle-brush Bush [previous page middle] or Scraggly Bottle-brush [previous]. Colonies may be solitary, but often grow in clusters. Shades of gray.

ABUNDANCE & DISTRIBUTION: Occasional to uncommon Florida, Bahamas, Caribbean.

HABITAT & BEHAVIOR: Inhabit deep reefs and drop-offs; occasionally in old shipwrecks.

NOTE: Positive identification requires microscopic examination. Pictured specimen collected (USNM 92279) at 90 feet, off West Palm Beach, Florida; visual identification confirmed in laboratory. Formerly classified in the genus Antipathes.

VISUAL ID: Colonies form long, single, unbranched, wire-like stalks that often twist and coil. May appear fuzzy, the result of polyp tentacles extending from stalk surfaces. Shades of yellow, yellow-brown, red-brown, brown and green. Without artificial light, some colonies appear chartreuse.

ABUNDANCE & DISTRIBUTION: Common South Florida, Bahamas, Caribbean.

HABITAT & BEHAVIOR: Inhabit a wide range of deep water environments, but most common in narrow, deep-cut canyons and along vertical wall faces. May appear as the predominant life form on some deep walls. Most abundant at depths over 90 feet.

NOTE: Originally described in the genus *Stichopathes* which was subsequently recognized as a subgenus of *Cirrhipathes*.

Wire Coral
Branch/polyp detail of red variation.

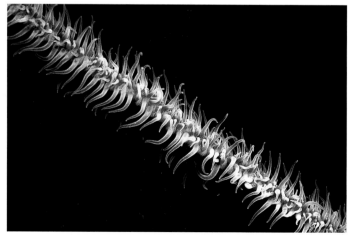

TURTLE GRASS
Thalassia testudinum
CLASS:
Angiospermae

SIZE: Length 4 - 24 in.
Width $^1/_8$ - $^1/_2$ in.
DEPTH: 3 - 65 ft.

Turtle Grass
Widely space plants,
mixed with manatee grass.
[next]

MANATEE GRASS
Syringodium filiforme
CLASS:
Angiospermae

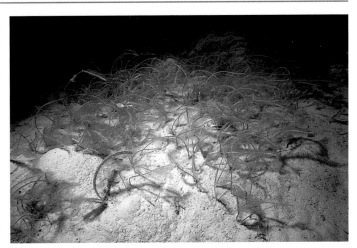

SIZE: Length 1$^1/_2$ - 18 in.
DEPTH: 3 - 40 ft.

Sea Grasses – Brown Algae

VISUAL ID: Generally erect, flat, elongated-oval, green leaves with distinctive midribs. Leaves of older, taller specimens are often rippled. Have extensive root system with well anchored runners. Leaves often covered with sediment and encrusting organisms.

ABUNDANCE & DISTRIBUTION: Occasional Florida, Bahamas, Caribbean.

HABITAT & BEHAVIOR: Grow in a wide range of habitats from muddy bottoms to sandy areas adjacent to reefs. May occur in areas of high sedimentation. Grow deeper than other sea grasses.

VISUAL ID: Individual plants join to form dense, relatively thick, floating mats that can cover huge areas of the sea surface. Thin, smooth, branching stems bear long, serrated blades and spherical, gas-filled floats that keep the plants on the surface. (Similar Sargasso Weed [next] distinguished by small spine or hook-like projection on floats). Light yellow-brown to golden brown to brown. Blades have distinctive central veins of lighter color.

ABUNDANCE & DISTRIBUTION: Abundant to common South Florida, Bahamas, Caribbean.

HABITAT & BEHAVIOR: Free floating on open sea surface. May form small clumps or huge rafts covering enormous areas of the ocean. Usually mixed with Sargasso Weed [next].

NOTE: Also commonly known as "Gulf Weed."

Sargassum Seaweed
Surface view of floating sargassum seaweed and sargasso weed.

MIDRIB SEAGRASS
Halophila baillonis
CLASS:
Angiospermae

SIZE: Length 1 - 2 in.
DEPTH: 12 - 90 ft.

SARGASSUM SEAWEED
Sargassum fluitans
PHYLUM:
Phaeophyta
Brown Algae

SIZE: ¹/₂ - 1¹/₂ ft.
DEPTH: 0 - 3 ft.

Sargassum Seaweed
*Large floating mat
of sargassum seaweed
and sargasso weed.*

Brown Algae

VISUAL ID: Individual plants join to form dense, relatively thick, floating mats that can cover huge areas of the sea surface. Thin, branching stems with small spines bear long, thin, serrated blades without prominent central veins. Spherical, gas-filled floats, tipped with small spines or hook-like projections, keep the plants on the surface. (Similar Sargassum Seaweed [previous] distinguished by floats without prominent spines and blades with obvious central veins.) Antique white to pale brown.

ABUNDANCE & DISTRIBUTION: Abundant to common South Florida, Bahamas, Caribbean.

HABITAT & BEHAVIOR: Free floating on open sea surface. May form small clumps or huge rafts covering enormous areas of the ocean. Usually mixed with Sargassum Seaweed [previous].

VISUAL ID: Several species of *Sargassum* attach to the substrate and grow in a bushy, upright form. Long, oval-shaped blades may have smooth or striated edges. Blades along with clusters of spherical gas-filled floats are attached to smooth, cylindrical stems. Whitish brown to brown, brown-green and olive. The similarity between species requires collection and laboratory examination for positive identification.

ABUNDANCE & DISTRIBUTION: Common to occasional South Florida, Bahamas, Caribbean.

HABITAT & BEHAVIOR: Grow in most environments, including reefs.

Sargassum Algae
Detail.

SARGASSO WEED
Sargassum natans
PHYLUM:
Phaeophyta
Brown Algae

SIZE: ½ - 1½ ft.
DEPTH: 0 - 3 ft.

SARGASSUM ALGAE
Sargassum sp.
PHYLUM:
Phaeophyta
Brown Algae

SIZE: 4 in. - 5 ft.
DEPTH: 1 - 100 ft.

Sargassum Algae
Growth pattern.

Brown Algae

VISUAL ID: Long, oval-shaped leaves are shades of brown to dark olive and distinctively marked with white central veins. Leaves attached to smooth, cylindrical stems. Can be somewhat bushy.

ABUNDANCE & DISTRIBUTION: Common to occasional South Florida, Bahamas, Caribbean.

HABITAT & BEHAVIOR: Grow in most environments, including reefs. Most common on deep patch reefs and surrounding areas of sand and rocky substrate.

VISUAL ID: There are several species in this genus difficult to distinguish visually, some described, others undescribed. All have branches that fork near their ends. Tips may be rounded or pointed. Generally they form mats of dense to loose packed flat leaves that overgrow the substrate. Light to medium brown and/or green to blue-green, occasionally with bright blue tints. Can spread to cover large areas.

ABUNDANCE & DISTRIBUTION: Abundant South Florida, Bahamas, Caribbean.

HABITAT & BEHAVIOR: Grow in most reef environments. Grow on rocky substrates, often covering boulders, around the base of coral heads, and on vertical wall faces. Most common in protected areas.

NOTE: Described species include *D. cervicornis, bartayresii, linearis* and *divaricata*.

 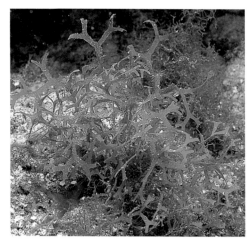

WHITE-VEIN SARGASSUM
Sargassum hystrix
PHYLUM:
Phaeophyta
Brown Algae

SIZE: 4 - 16 in.
DEPTH: 30 - 330 ft.

Y BRANCHED ALGAE
Dictyota sp.
PHYLUM:
Phaeophyta
Brown Algae

SIZE: 4 - 18 in.
DEPTH: 0 - 200 ft.

Y Branched Algae
Color and growth patterns.

VISUAL ID: Bushy clumps of strap-like blades that have distinctive points along their edges. Irregularly branched dichotomously. Light yellow-brown to brown, with light, wavy pattern; may have greenish tints.

ABUNDANCE & DISTRIBUTION: Abundant South Florida, Bahamas, Caribbean.

HABITAT & BEHAVIOR: Grow in most reef environments. Attach to rocky substrates, often in exposed areas with surge.

SIMILAR SPECIES: Smooth Strap Algae, *D. dichotoma,* distinguished by thin, dichotomously branched blades with smooth edges.

VISUAL ID: Bushy plant formed by flat, squared-off blades that are irregularly branched and split. Concentrically banded in a wide range of colors, including shades of yellow, yellow-green, green, brown-green, brown, and often with tints of iridescent green and/or blue.

ABUNDANCE & DISTRIBUTION: Abundant to occasional South Florida, Bahamas, Caribbean.

HABITAT & BEHAVIOR: Attach to rocky substrate in most reef environments. Often abundant in shallow water less than five feet, only occasional to rare on deeper reefs.

Leafy Flat-blade Alga
Color variation.

SERRATED STRAP ALGA
Dictyota ciliolata
PHYLUM:
Phaeophyta
Brown Algae

SIZE: 4 - 6 in.
DEPTH: 0 - 35 ft.

LEAFY FLAT-BLADE ALGA
Stypopodium zonale
PHYLUM:
Phaeophyta
Brown Algae

SIZE: Blade length
31/2 - 16 in.
DEPTH: 0 - 260 ft.

Leafy Flat-blade Alga
Color variation.

Brown Algae

VISUAL ID: Form large, dense clumps of leafy blades with rounded, often semicircular outer margins. Blades are irregularly split and branched. Concentrically banded in a wide range of colors, including shades of yellow, yellow-green, green, brown-green, brown, and often with tints of iridescent green and/or blue. Outer margins are often of lighter color.

ABUNDANCE & DISTRIBUTION: Abundant to occasional South Florida, Bahamas, Caribbean.

HABITAT & BEHAVIOR: Attach to rocky substrate in most reef environments. Often abundant in shallow water less than five feet, while only occasional to rare on deeper reefs.

NOTE: Identification tentative; members of this genus require sectioning near the base and microscopic examination for positive identification. Formerly classified as *P. gymnospora.*

VISUAL ID: Form large, dense clumps of leafy blades with rounded, often semicircular, outer margins. Blades are irregularly split and branched. Concentrically banded in shades of white to grayish white, tan and light yellowish brown.

ABUNDANCE & DISTRIBUTION: Abundant to occasional South Florida, Bahamas, Caribbean.

HABITAT & BEHAVIOR: Attach to rocky substrates in most marine environments, especially shallow reef flats.

NOTE: Identification tentative; members of this genus require sectioning near the base and microscopic examination for positive identification. Formerly classified as *P. sanctae-crucis.*

VISUAL ID: Thin, fan-shaped blades encrust substrate, often overlapping in a shingle-like pattern. Shades of green-brown to tan to brown.

ABUNDANCE & DISTRIBUTION: Abundant to common South Florida, Bahamas, Caribbean.

HABITAT & BEHAVIOR: Grow in most reef environments, encrusting great areas of shaded, rocky substrate. Especially abundant on undercut wall faces along deep drop-offs. Blade surfaces often covered with sediment and encrusted with other growths (epiphytes).

NOTE: This species has two additional growth forms; both grow in shallow to intertidal water and rarely on reefs. The blades of both forms are less flattened and more ruffled and range in color from light green to orange-brown.

LEAFY ROLLED-BLADE ALGA
Padina boergesenii
PHYLUM:
Phaeophyta
Brown Algae

SIZE: Blade length
4 - 6 in.
DEPTH: 0 - 50 ft.

WHITE SCROLL ALGA
Padina jamaicensis
PHYLUM:
Phaeophyta
Brown Algae

SIZE: Blade height
2 ½ - 6 in.
DEPTH: 0 - 50 ft.

ENCRUSTING FAN-LEAF ALGA
Lobophora variegata
PHYLUM:
Phaeophyta
Brown Algae

SIZE: Blade diameter
1 - 6 in.
DEPTH: 12 - 350 ft.

Brown Algae

VISUAL ID: A spongy-looking mass of tangled, interconnected branches with numerous irregularly sized holes. Has no permanent holdfasts and can form large masses. Very pale brown to light yellow-brown. May fluoresce dayglow orange which disappears when illuminated by a hand light or strobe.

ABUNDANCE & DISTRIBUTION: Abundant to common Florida; occasional to rare Bahamas, Caribbean.

HABITAT & BEHAVIOR: Grow in most reef environments. May move about in current, coming to rest in shallow depressions or where the mass hooks on or around various bottom growths or outcroppings.

VISUAL ID: Erect central column with branches bearing clumps of triangular, cone-shaped blades with saucer-like tips. (Similar Blistered Saucer Leaf Alga [next] leaf tips have swollen centers.) Short, sharp spines extend from blade stalk. Brownish cream to tan to brown, often with dark brown speckles.

ABUNDANCE & DISTRIBUTION: Occasional Florida, Bahamas, Caribbean.

HABITAT & BEHAVIOR: Grow in shallow intertidal zones to shallow lagoons and back reef areas with moderate to strong water movement.

NOTE: This species and Blistered Saucer Leaf Alga [next] are so similar in appearance that positive identification requires collection and laboratory examination.

VISUAL ID: Erect central column with branches bearing clumps of triangular, cone-shaped blades with saucer-like tips. A blister-like swelling at center of leaf tips is the result of an embedded air bladder that holds the leaves and plant erect (compare similar Saucer Leaf Alga [previous]). Brownish cream to tan to brown, often with dark brown speckles.

ABUNDANCE & DISTRIBUTION: Occasional Florida, Bahamas, Caribbean.

HABITAT & BEHAVIOR: Grow in shallow intertidal zones to shallow lagoons and back reef areas with moderate to strong water movement.

NOTE: This species and Saucer Leaf Alga [previous] are so similar in appearance that positive identification requires collection and laboratory examination.

SWISS CHEESE ALGA
Hydroclathrus clathratus
PHYLUM:
Phaeophyta
Brown Algae

SIZE: 3 in. - 3 ft.
DEPTH: 10 - 60 ft.

SAUCER LEAF ALGA
Turbinaria tricostata
PHYLUM:
Phaeophyta
Brown Algae

SIZE: 4 - 16 in.
DEPTH: 0 - 20 ft.

BLISTERED
SAUCER LEAF ALGA
Turbinaria turbinata
PHYLUM:
Phaeophyta
Brown Algae

SIZE: 4 - 16 in.
DEPTH: 0 - 20 ft.

Green Algae

VISUAL ID: Thick, profusely branched clumps of rounded, three-lobed or ribbed, leaf-like segments. Spread laterally to cover large areas of reef or sand. Dark to bright green and yellowish green.

ABUNDANCE & DISTRIBUTION: Abundant South Florida, Bahamas, Caribbean.

HABITAT & BEHAVIOR: Grow in shallow depressions, cracks and crevices, between hard corals and other somewhat protected areas of the reef. Also grow on sand, especially around and on reefs.

NOTE: The calcified leaves of this and other species of *Halimeda* are considered major contributors of calcium carbonate to the reefs and sand.

Watercress Alga
Occasionally covers large areas of reef.

VISUAL ID: Branched clumps of rounded, smooth, fan- or disk-shaped, leaf-like segments. Attached by single, short holdfast with flexible joints between segments. Tend to grow in single plane (less obvious in larger plants). Bright green to yellowish green, occasionally white; segment edges often yellow. Leaf-like segments are the largest found in this genus.

ABUNDANCE & DISTRIBUTION: Abundant to common South Florida, Bahamas, Caribbean.

HABITAT & BEHAVIOR: Grow in most marine environments from reefs to flat bottom plains of sand, rubble and hard substrates.

NOTE: The calcified leaves of this and other species of *Halimeda* are considered major contributors of calcium carbonate to the reefs and sand.

WATERCRESS ALGA
Halimeda opuntia

PHYLUM:
Chlorophyta
Green Algae

SIZE: 4 - 8 in.
Segment width $^1/_8$ - $^3/_8$ in.
DEPTH: 3 - 150 ft.

Watercress Alga
Note white calcareous structure of dead segments.

LARGE LEAF WATERCRESS ALGA
Halimeda discoidea

PHYLUM:
Chlorophyta
Green Algae

SIZE: 4 - 8 in.
Segment width $^3/_8$ - $1^1/_2$ in.
DEPTH: 3 - 220 ft.

Green Algae

VISUAL ID: Branched clumps of thin, rounded, fan- or disk-shaped, leaf-like segments. Attached by stalk formed of basal segments, especially noticeable in older plants. Young tend to grow in single plane, becoming somewhat bushy with age. Bright green to yellowish green, and green.

ABUNDANCE & DISTRIBUTION: Abundant to common South Florida, Bahamas, Caribbean.

HABITAT & BEHAVIOR: Grow in most marine environments from reefs to flat bottom plains of sand, rubble and hard substrates.

NOTE: The calcified leaves of this and other species of *Halimeda* are considered major contributors of calcium carbonate to the reefs and sand.

VISUAL ID: Chains of spherical or bulbous segments, resembling strings of beads, without distinct stalk. Pale green to whitish.

ABUNDANCE & DISTRIBUTION: Common to occasional South Florida, Bahamas, Cuba. Not reported Caribbean.

HABITAT & BEHAVIOR: Grow on reefs and rocky substrates.

NOTE: The calcified leaves of this and other species of *Halimeda* are considered major contributors of calcium carbonate to the reefs and sand.

VISUAL ID: Long chain of rounded, three-lobed, relatively small, leaf-like segments held together by a thin strand running through their centers. Rare to occasional branching of strands. Bright green to yellowish green.

ABUNDANCE & DISTRIBUTION: Abundant to common South Florida, Bahamas, Caribbean.

HABITAT & BEHAVIOR: Tend to grow in shaded areas of reef, often hanging from ledge undercuts and along walls.

NOTE: The calcified leaves of this and other species of *Halimeda* are considered major contributors of calcium carbonate to the reefs and sand.

STALKED LETTUCE LEAF ALGA
Halimeda tuna
PHYLUM:
Chlorophyta
Green Algae

SIZE: 4 - 10 in.
Segment width $^1/_2$ - $^3/_4$ in.
DEPTH: 30 - 220 ft.

BULBOUS LETTUCE LEAF ALGA
Halimeda lacrimosa
PHYLUM:
Chlorophyta
Green Algae

SIZE: Height 1 - 2 in.
Chain length to 10 in.
Segment diameter $^1/_4$ in.
DEPTH: 3 - 280 ft.

SMALL-LEAF HANGING VINE
Halimeda goreaui
PHYLUM:
Chlorophyta
Green Algae

SIZE: Strand length
6 - 12 in.
Segment width $^1/_8$ - $^1/_4$ in.
DEPTH: 30 - 250 ft.

Green Algae

VISUAL ID: Long chain of rectangular-shaped, relatively large, leaf-like segments held together by a thin strand running through their centers. Strands may branch frequently. Bright green to yellowish green on top, underside often lighter.

ABUNDANCE & DISTRIBUTION: Abundant to common South Florida, Bahamas, Caribbean.

HABITAT & BEHAVIOR: Tend to grow in shaded areas of reef, often hanging from ledge undercuts and along walls.

NOTE: The calcified leaves of this and other species of *Halimeda* are considered major contributors of calcium carbonate to the reefs and sand.

VISUAL ID: Upright, occasionally branched, chains of distinctly three-lobed or ribbed, leaf-like segments. Stiff, primary stalk composed of united segments. Dark to bright green to yellowish green.

ABUNDANCE & DISTRIBUTION: Abundant to common South Florida, Bahamas, Caribbean.

HABITAT & BEHAVIOR: Most commonly inhabit shallow sandy areas, including sea grass beds. Occasionally in sandy, rocky areas on and between reefs.

NOTE: The calcified leaves of this and other species of *Halimeda* are considered major contributors of calcium carbonate to the reefs and sand.

LARGE-LEAF HANGING VINE
Halimeda copiosa
PHYLUM:
Chlorophyta
Green Algae

SIZE: Strand length
4 - 24 in.
Segment width ½ - ¾ in.
DEPTH: 50 - 200 ft.

Large-leaf Hanging Vine
Detail of leaf-like segments.

THREE FINGER LEAF ALGA
Halimeda incrassata
PHYLUM:
Chlorophyta
Green Algae

SIZE: Height 4 - 10 in.
DEPTH: 3 - 40 ft.

Green Algae

VISUAL ID: Upright, occasionally branched, chains of cylindrical to somewhat flattened segments. Branching occurs from three-lobed segments. Relatively stiff structure. Dark to bright green to yellowish green.

ABUNDANCE & DISTRIBUTION: Occasional South Florida, Bahamas, Caribbean.

HABITAT & BEHAVIOR: Most commonly inhabit shallow sandy areas, including sea grass beds. Occasionally in sandy, rocky areas on and between reefs.

NOTE: The calcified leaves of this and other species of *Halimeda* are considered major contributors of calcium carbonate to the reefs and sand.

VISUAL ID: Cone-shaped with flattish top. Tip of cone merges into a heavy, short stalk anchored in sand. Composed of tightly packed, bristle-like filaments. Dark green to gray-green.

ABUNDANCE & DISTRIBUTION: Occasional South Florida, Bahamas, Caribbean.

HABITAT & BEHAVIOR: Grow in sandy, protected areas, often on and between reefs.

NOTE: Identification probable, positive identification requires collection and laboratory examination.

VISUAL ID: Spherical ball of tightly packed bristle-like filaments that merge into a heavy, short stalk anchored in sand. Composed of tightly packed, bristle-like filaments. Dark green to gray-green.

ABUNDANCE & DISTRIBUTION: Occasional South Florida, Bahamas, Caribbean.

HABITAT & BEHAVIOR: Grow in sandy, protected areas, often on and between reefs.

GREEN JOINTED-STALK ALGA
Halimeda monile
PHYLUM:
Chlorophyta
Green Algae

SIZE: Height 3 - 8 in.
DEPTH: 3 - 40 ft.

FLAT-TOP BRISTLE BRUSH
Penicillus pyriformis
PHYLUM:
Chlorophyta
Green Algae

SIZE: 2 - 4 ½ in.
DEPTH: 3 - 100 ft.

BRISTLE BALL BRUSH
Penicillus dumetosus
PHYLUM:
Chlorophyta
Green Algae

SIZE: 2 - 6 in.
DEPTH: 6 - 50 ft.

211

Green Algae

VISUAL ID: Tall, stiff, feather-like structures grow upward from long, cylindrical, attached runners. Pinnate branchlets are cylindrical with sharp points. Light green.

ABUNDANCE & DISTRIBUTION: Occasional South Florida, Bahamas, Caribbean.

HABITAT & BEHAVIOR: Grow in shallow sandy areas, often between protected shallow reefs. Also grow in areas of mangroves and occasionally attach to their roots.

VISUAL ID: Flat feather-like structures grow upward from long, cylindrical, attached runners. Pinnate branchlets have sharp points and taper into the midrib. Yellow-green to green.

ABUNDANCE & DISTRIBUTION: Occasional South Florida, Bahamas, Caribbean.

HABITAT & BEHAVIOR: Grow in shallow to moderate depths in sandy areas and on rocky reefs. Also grow in areas of mangroves and occasionally attach to their roots. In shallow areas with surge, tend to be short (about 1-3 inches); reach maximum height in deeper protected areas.

VISUAL ID: Small serrated blades with edges grow upward from long, cylindrical, attached runners. Blades often fork and are occasionally twisted. Shades of light to medium mint green, often with bluish tints.

ABUNDANCE & DISTRIBUTION: Occasional South Florida, Bahamas, Caribbean.

HABITAT & BEHAVIOR: Grow in shallow rocky substrates, usually with some sand covering. Often adjacent to protected back patch and fringing reefs.

GREEN FEATHER ALGA
Caulerpa sertularioides

PHYLUM:
Chlorophyta
Green Algae

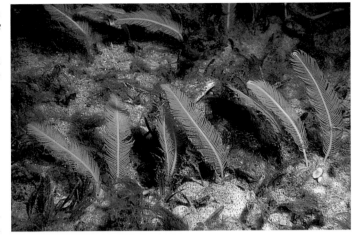

SIZE: 4 - 8 in.
DEPTH: 3 - 35 ft.

FLAT GREEN FEATHER ALGA
Caulerpa mexicana

PHYLUM:
Chlorophyta
Green Algae

SIZE: 1 - 8 in.
DEPTH: 3 - 50 ft.

SAW-BLADE ALGA
Caulerpa serrulata

PHYLUM:
Chlorophyta
Green Algae

SIZE: Blades $3/4$ - $1 1/2$ in.
DEPTH: 3 - 18 ft.

Green Algae

VISUAL ID: Small, flat, elongated, oval blades with short, cylindrical stalks. Additional blades may branch off from stalk. Grow upward from long, cylindrical, attached runners. Yellow-green to green and dark green.

ABUNDANCE & DISTRIBUTION: Occasional South Florida, Bahamas, Caribbean.

HABITAT & BEHAVIOR: Grow in sandy areas, often adjacent to shallow patch reefs. May mix with Turtle Grass[pg. 191].

VISUAL ID: Numerous, long, branching, cylindrical runners bear clusters of grape-like spheres attached by tiny stem-like branchlets. Shades of light to medium green, often with bluish tints. Somewhat different growth patterns of this species, var. *peltata*, have disk-like appendages attached to the branchlets; var. *macrophyso*, form upright columns bearing grape-like spheres.

ABUNDANCE & DISTRIBUTION: Common South Florida, Bahamas, Caribbean.

HABITAT & BEHAVIOR: Most commonly grow in intertidal to shallow rocky areas, usually with at least some surge and water movement. Also inhabit rocky areas of shallow to moderately deep reefs. Several species of nudibranchs feed exclusively on this alga.

Green Grape Alga
Upright column growth pattern, var. macrophyso.

OVAL-BLADE ALGA
Caulerpa prolifera

PHYLUM:
Chlorophyta
Green Algae

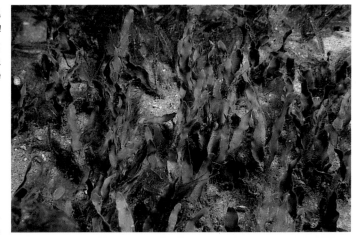

SIZE: Blades 2 - 4 in.
DEPTH: 3 - 50 ft.

GREEN GRAPE ALGA
Caulerpa racemosa

PHYLUM:
Chlorophyta
Green Algae

SIZE: $^1/_2$ - 6 in.
DEPTH: 0 - 65 ft.

Green Grape Alga
*Disk-shaped tip growth
pattern, var.* peltata.

Green Algae

VISUAL ID: Trunk-like stalks that divide into thick, heavy, upright branches extend from sand covered runners. Branches lined with long rows of short, thick, variously shaped branchlets. May be tall and slender with only a few branches, or short and bushy with numerous branches.

ABUNDANCE & DISTRIBUTION: Occasional South Florida, Bahamas, Caribbean. Can be abundant in localized areas.

HABITAT & BEHAVIOR: Grow in shallow, protected sandy areas, often adjacent to back patch and fringing reefs.

SIMILAR SPECIES: Tall Cactus Alga, *C. lanuginosa,* single, unbranched columns (3-5 in.) grow upward from sand-covered runners.

VISUAL ID: Small, cylindrical, ringed stalks with fuzzy tips. May grow singly or in compact clumps. Tips green; stalks white with greenish tints.

ABUNDANCE & DISTRIBUTION: Occasional South Florida, Bahamas, Caribbean. Can be abundant in localized areas.

HABITAT & BEHAVIOR: Grow on sandy, rocky substrates and areas of coral rubble. Occasionally on reefs. Often in shaded areas.

VISUAL ID: Clusters of cylindrical branches composed of fine, tightly compacted branchlets. Olive to dark green.

ABUNDANCE & DISTRIBUTION: Occasional South Florida, Bahamas, Caribbean.

HABITAT & BEHAVIOR: Grow in a variety of shallow water habitats, from mangrove areas to tidal pools to shallow reefs. Attach to hard substrates.

NOTE: Identification probable, positive identification requires collection and magnified examination of branchlet filaments.

CACTUS TREE ALGA
Caulerpa cupressoides

PHYLUM:
Chlorophyta
Green Algae

SIZE: Height 1 - 10 in.
DEPTH: 3 - 18 ft.

FUZZY TIP ALGA
Neomeris annulata

PHYLUM:
Chlorophyta
Green Algae

SIZE: Height ³/₄ - 1¹/₄ in.
DEPTH: 0 - 100 ft.

FUZZY FINGER ALGA
Dasycladus vermicularis

PHYLUM:
Chlorophyta
Green Algae

SIZE: Height 1 - 2¹/₂ in.
DEPTH: 0 - 25 ft.

Green Algae

VISUAL ID: Bushy, hemispherical growths of cylindrical branches with fine, hair-like covering. Branch tips often dichotomously branched. Pale to medium green.

ABUNDANCE & DISTRIBUTION: Occasional South Florida, Bahamas, Caribbean.

HABITAT & BEHAVIOR: Grow on rocky substrates, occasionally on reefs. Most common in shallow areas between 5-25 feet.

VISUAL ID: Dark green spheres with bright reflective sheen. Often covered with thin, silvery to light lavender algae. Attached to substrate by fine, hair-like runners. One of the largest single cells found in either the Plant or Animal Kingdoms.

ABUNDANCE & DISTRIBUTION: Common to occasional South Florida, Bahamas, Caribbean.

HABITAT & BEHAVIOR: Grow in most reef environments, often in small cracks and crevices mixed with other algae. Tend to be solitary, but occasionally in small groups. May be encrusted with tunicates and other organisms.

VISUAL ID: Dark green bubble-like cells with bright, reflective, silvery sheen. Range from spheres to elongated ovals. Grow in tightly compacted, mat-like clusters.

ABUNDANCE & DISTRIBUTION: Common South Florida, Bahamas, Caribbean.

HABITAT & BEHAVIOR: Inhabit most reef environments, especially in protected, shaded areas, such as under ledge overhangs and in cracks. Often overgrown by other organisms. More common on shallow reefs, but also occurs much deeper.

NOTE: There are several similar appearing species of *Valonia* and identification is tentative. Positive identification requires laboratory examination of collected specimen.

DEAD MAN'S FINGERS
Codium isthmocladum
PHYLUM:
Chlorophyta
Green Algae

SIZE: Height 4 - 8 in.
DEPTH: 3 - 80 ft.

SEA PEARL
Ventricaria ventricosa
PHYLUM:
Chlorophyta
Green Algae

SIZE: Diameter
$^3/_4$ - 2 in.
DEPTH: 3 - 250 ft.

ELONGATED SEA PEARLS
Valonia macrophysa
PHYLUM:
Chlorophyta
Green Algae

SIZE: Diameter
$^1/_4$ - $^3/_4$ in.
DEPTH: 3 - 140 ft.

Green Algae

VISUAL ID: Clusters of dark green, bubble-like cells grow in spreading runners. Do not form dense mats as Elongated Sea Pearls [previous]. Shapes range from spheres to elongated ovals. Outgrowths are occasionally erect.

ABUNDANCE & DISTRIBUTION: Occasional South Florida, Bahamas, Caribbean.

HABITAT & BEHAVIOR: Inhabit most reef environments, especially in protected, shaded areas, such as under ledge overhangs and in cracks. Most common on shallow reefs, but also occur much deeper.

NOTE: There are several similar appearing species of *Valonia* and identification is tentative. Positive identification requires laboratory examination of collected specimen.

VISUAL ID: Spherical to irregularly lobed clumps. Walls composed of small bubble-like cells giving the surface a cobblestone-like texture. Shades of light green.

ABUNDANCE & DISTRIBUTION: Common to occasional South Florida, Bahamas, Caribbean.

HABITAT & BEHAVIOR: Grow in most reef environments, attaching to rocky substrates and areas of dead coral. On occasion cover extensive areas. Can be abundant in localized areas, especially with high nutrient levels.

VISUAL ID: Thin, rounded, upright blades composed of long vertical veins that divide at their tips into sprays of smaller veins, reminiscent of papyrus grass. Large, elongated cells lay parallel to one another between, and perpendicular to, the veins. Shades of bright green to yellowish green.

ABUNDANCE & DISTRIBUTION: Occasional South Florida, Bahamas, Caribbean.

HABITAT & BEHAVIOR: Grow in shaded, protected, rocky areas such as under ledge overhangs and in cracks and crevices.

CREEPING BUBBLE ALGA
Valonia utricularis
PHYLUM:
Chlorophyta
Green Algae

SIZE: Diameter $1/4$ in.
Length to 1 in.
DEPTH: 3 - 100 ft.

GREEN BUBBLE WEED
Dictyosphaeria cavernosa
PHYLUM:
Chlorophyta
Green Algae

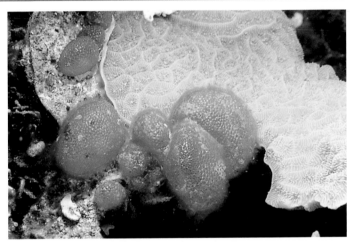

SIZE: $1^1/4$ - 8 in.
DEPTH: 3 - 100 ft.

PAPYRUS PRINT ALGA
Anadyomene stellata
PHYLUM:
Chlorophyta
Green Algae

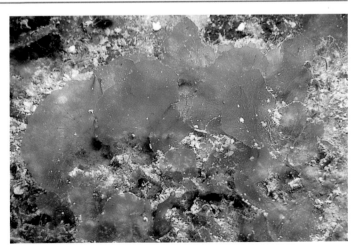

SIZE: $1^1/4$ - 4 in.
DEPTH: 0 - 100 ft.

Green Algae

VISUAL ID: Clumps of thin, stiff, crumpled blades composed of a tight, rough network of long, large filaments. Pale to dark green.

ABUNDANCE & DISTRIBUTION: Occasional South Florida, Bahamas, Caribbean.

HABITAT & BEHAVIOR: Grow in open areas of reef attached to hard substrate. Often in environments with some light sedimentation.

Network Alga
Close-up: note network structure.

VISUAL ID: Tangled masses formed by a somewhat stiff network of long, fine filaments. Pale to dark green.

ABUNDANCE & DISTRIBUTION: Occasional Caribbean.

HABITAT & BEHAVIOR: Grow in most marine environments, more common in areas with little water movement. May attach in small clumps or grow in masses of considerable size, covering large areas of substrate.

NOTE: Visual identification probable, positive identification requires microscopic examination of collected specimen.

NETWORK ALGA
Microdictyon marinum
PHYLUM:
Chlorophyta
Green Algae

SIZE: 1¼ - 4 in.
DEPTH: 3 - 50 ft.

Network Alga
Detail of filament structure.

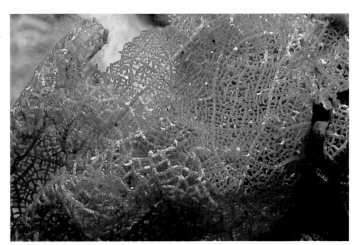

GREEN NET ALGA
Microdictyon boergesenii
PHYLUM:
Chlorophyta
Green Algae

SIZE: 1¼ in. to several ft.
DEPTH: 3 - 100 ft.

continued next page 223

Green Algae

Green Net Alga
Close-up of network.

VISUAL ID: Fan-shaped blades with smooth edges and surface texture. Rounded bottom of blades turn in and upward to stem. Stems attached to long slender runners. Dark green to grayish green.

ABUNDANCE & DISTRIBUTION: Common to occasional South Florida, Bahamas, Caribbean.

HABITAT & BEHAVIOR: Grow in sandy areas, on and between reefs. In shallow areas with water movement, often in rows on short stalks. In deeper, calm water, often grow tall and singly or in small clusters.

NOTE: Identification probable, positive identification requires laboratory examination of collected specimen.

VISUAL ID: Paddle-shaped blades with relatively smooth edges and surface texture. Stems attached to large bulbous holdfast. Dark green to grayish green.

ABUNDANCE & DISTRIBUTION: Common to occasional South Florida, Bahamas, Caribbean.

HABITAT & BEHAVIOR: Grow in sandy areas, on and between reefs. In shallow areas with water movement, often in rows on short stalks. In deeper, calm water, often grow tall and singly or in small clusters.

NOTE: Identification probable, positive identification requires laboratory examination of collected specimen.

Green Net Alga
*continued from
previous page*

Detail of structure.

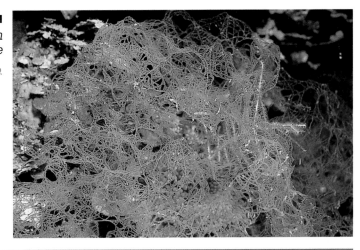

SAUCER BLADE ALGA
Avrainvillea asarifolia
PHYLUM:
Chlorophyta
Green Algae

SIZE: Blade height
1 1/2- 6 in.
Stalk 1 - 12 in.
DEPTH: 3 - 120 ft.

PADDLE BLADE ALGA
Avrainvillea longicaulis
PHYLUM:
Chlorophyta
Green Algae

SIZE: Blade height
1 1/2 - 4 in.
Stalk 1 - 8 in.
DEPTH: 3 - 100 ft.

Green Algae

VISUAL ID: Several species in this genus have broad, fan-shaped blades attached to single stalks. They are heavily calcified, stiff and erect. Lines (thin filament ridges) extend radially from point of stem attachments to edge. Many have one or more concentric lines or zones on blades' surfaces. Whitish green to yellow-green, medium green and dark green. Because of their similarity in appearance, positive identification to species requires magnified examination of blade filaments.

ABUNDANCE & DISTRIBUTION: Common South Florida, Bahamas, Caribbean.

HABITAT & BEHAVIOR: Grow in sandy, protected areas, on and between reefs and areas of coral rubble. Usually grow in groups.

NOTE: Based on visual appearance of overall structure, opposite is possibly *U. flabellum,* middle right may be *U. spinulosa,* and bottom right may be *U. wilsonii.*

Mermaid's Fans
Growth pattern.

Mermaid's Fans
Growth pattern.

MERMAID'S FANS
Udotea sp.
PHYLUM:
Chlorophyta
Green Algae

SIZE: Height 1 - 8 in.
DEPTH: 0 - 120 ft.

Mermaid's Fans
Growth pattern.

Mermaid's Fans
Growth pattern.

Green Algae

VISUAL ID: Paper-thin cup attached to a small, single stalk anchored in sand. Quite delicate, structure often torn. Medium green to whitish green.

ABUNDANCE & DISTRIBUTION: Occasional South Florida, Bahamas, Caribbean.

HABITAT & BEHAVIOR: Grow in sandy, protected areas, on and between reefs and in areas of coral rubble. Usually grow in groups.

VISUAL ID: Pinecone-shaped, composed of tightly-packed flattened blades growing upward and concentrically from a single stalk. Green to mint green and whitish green. There are two additional distinctive growth patterns of this species. Form *brevifolius* has a thin, elongated pinecone shape. Form *longifolius* has ragged, more loosely arranged blades and a somewhat flattened top.

ABUNDANCE & DISTRIBUTION: Occasional South Florida, Bahamas, Caribbean.

HABITAT & BEHAVIOR: Most commonly inhabit shallow sandy areas, including sea grass beds. Occasionally in sandy, rocky areas on and between reefs.

Pinecone Alga
*Elongate Pinecone Alga
form* brevifolius.

MERMAID'S TEA CUP
Udotea cyathiformis
PHYLUM:
Chlorophyta
Green Algae

SIZE: Cup height 2 - 6 in.
DEPTH: 3 - 100 ft.

PINECONE ALGA
Rhipocephalus phoenix
PHYLUM:
Chlorophyta
Green Algae

SIZE: Height 2 - 5 in.
DEPTH: 3 - 150 ft.

Pinecone Alga
*Ragged Pinecone Alga
form* longifolius.

VISUAL ID: Round, saucer-shaped caps on long, thin stalks. Ruffled rays radiate from centers, with a small spine at the tip of each ray. White with slight greenish tint.

ABUNDANCE & DISTRIBUTION: Occasional South Florida, Bahamas, Caribbean.

HABITAT & BEHAVIOR: Grow in shallow protected areas of reef, areas of coral rubble, adjacent sea grass beds and mangrove areas. May grow solitary or in groups.

NOTE: Visual identification probable, positive identification requires laboratory examination of collected specimen.

VISUAL ID: Clumps of round, saucer-shaped caps on long thin stalks. Ruffled rays radiate from centers to edges. Pale green to yellowish green.

ABUNDANCE & DISTRIBUTION: Occasional South Florida, Bahamas, Caribbean.

HABITAT & BEHAVIOR: Grow in shallow protected areas of reef, areas of coral rubble, adjacent sea grass beds, sand flats and mangrove areas. Usually in clumps, rarely solitary.

NOTE: Visual identification probable, positive identification requires laboratory examination of collected specimen.

VISUAL ID: Light pink color is distinctive of these tall, bushy clumps. Small branches extend alternately from either side of main branches (in a single plane).

ABUNDANCE & DISTRIBUTION: Common to occasional Florida, Bahamas, Caribbean.

HABITAT & BEHAVIOR: Grow in most marine environments from shallow to moderate depths. Attach to nearly any hard substrate.

NOTE: Visual identification probable, positive identification requires laboratory examination of collected specimen.

WHITE MERMAID'S WINE GLASS
Acetabularia crenulata

PHYLUM:
Chlorophyta
Green Algae

SIZE: Height
³/₄ - 3 ¹/₄ in.
Cap Diameter
¹/₄ - ³/₄ in.
DEPTH: 3 - 20 ft.

GREEN MERMAID'S WINE GLASS
Acetabularia calyculus

PHYLUM:
Chlorophyta
Green Algae

SIZE: Height
¹/₂ - 1¹/₂ in.
Cap Diameter
¹/₄ in.
DEPTH: 1 - 18 ft.

PINK BUSH ALGA
Wrangelia penicillata

PHYLUM:
Rhodophyta
Red Algae

SIZE: 4 - 8 in.
DEPTH: 3 - 50 ft.

Red Algae

VISUAL ID: Several members of this genus cannot be distinguished visually and require laboratory examination for positive identification. In general their segments profusely branch dichotomously forming dense hemispherical domes attached by a single holdfast. Segments are tubular, smooth and relatively hard (heavily calcified) with flexible joints. Branch tips appear crosscut and have a central hole. Reddish to orangish and off-white.

ABUNDANCE & DISTRIBUTION: Common to occasional Florida, Bahamas, Caribbean.

HABITAT & BEHAVIOR: Generally inhabit protected areas of sand and rocks or rocky substrates, occasionally on shallow patch reefs. Attach to rocks and other hard substrates.

Tubular Thicket Algae
Growth pattern and color variation.

VISUAL ID: Grow in tangled, small clumps. Wide, dichotomously branched structures composed of rigid, stony, cylindrical segments and flexible joints. Segments light red to pink; joints white.

ABUNDANCE & DISTRIBUTION: Occasional Florida, Bahamas, Caribbean.

HABITAT & BEHAVIOR: Generally inhabit protected, somewhat shaded areas of reef. Often fill small cracks, nooks and depressions in rocky substrate.

NOTE: Visual identification probable, positive identification requires laboratory examination of collected specimen.

TUBULAR THICKET ALGAE
Galaxaura sp.

PHYLUM:
Rhodophyta
Red Algae

SIZE: 4 - 6 in.
DEPTH: 3 - 40 ft.

Tubular Thicket Algae
Growth pattern and color variation.

PINK SEGMENTED ALGA
Jania adherens

PHYLUM
Rhodophyta
Red Algae

SIZE: Height 1 - 2 in.
DEPTH: 0 - 60 ft.

Red Algae

VISUAL ID: Grow in tangled, small clumps. Randomly branched structures composed of stony, flat, thin segments. Flexible, obscure joints at forks of branches. Whitish with light red to pink tinting.

ABUNDANCE & DISTRIBUTION: Occasional Florida, Bahamas, Caribbean.

HABITAT & BEHAVIOR: Primarily inhabit reef crests and fore reefs. Generally in protected, somewhat shaded areas. May fill small cracks, nooks and depressions in rocky substrate.

VISUAL ID: Grow in tangled, small clumps formed of widely spaced, stony, thin, cylindrical, dichotomously forked branches. Flexible joints are obscure and rarely occur at forks. Whitish, often with light red to pink tinting.

ABUNDANCE & DISTRIBUTION: Occasional Florida, Bahamas, Caribbean.

HABITAT & BEHAVIOR: Often grow in shallow grass beds. Also inhabit reefs, generally in protected, somewhat shaded areas. May fill small cracks, nooks and depressions in rocky substrate.

SIMILAR SPECIES: *A. brasiliana* distinguished by pink color, somewhat flattened and more tightly bunched branches. *A. fragilissima* distinguished by swollen segment ends and wide angle of dichotomous branching forming thickly tangled clumps.

VISUAL ID: Thin, hard, highly calcified encrustations overgrowing rocky, limestone substrates. Take on surface texture of substrate. Shades of pinkish gray.

ABUNDANCE & DISTRIBUTION: Abundant to common Florida Keys, Bahamas, Caribbean.

HABITAT & BEHAVIOR: Most common on subtidal to intertidal reef crests where it can cover huge areas. Often in areas of clustered small holes, bored by chitons, *Acanthochitona lata,* that feed on other algae. Very important reef building element, acting as a cement-like covering and adhesive that protects the structure from the destructive elements of strong surge and breaking waves.

FLAT TWIG ALGA
Amphiroa tribulus

PHYLUM
Rhodophyta
Red Algae

SIZE: Height 1 - 4 in.
DEPTH: 0 - 40 ft.

Y-TWIG ALGA
Amphiroa rigida

PHYLUM
Rhodophyta
Red Algae

SIZE: Height 3 - 6 in.
DEPTH: 0 - 60 ft.

REEF CEMENT
Porolithon pachydermum

PHYLUM:
Rhodophyta
Red Algae

SIZE: N/A
DEPTH: 0 - 30 ft.

Red Algae

VISUAL ID: There are a number of species in several genera that generally form thin, brittle, highly calcified encrustations and rounded plates. Occasionally their outer edges extend outward from substrate. They are usually dark red to burgundy, violet, lavender or pink, often with thin white margins. May be quite fragile, especially along extended edges. Colonies are so individually variable in appearance, and yet similar to one another, that they cannot easily be distinguished visually. Positive identification requires laboratory examination that includes decalcification, sectioning and microscopic examination.

ABUNDANCE & DISTRIBUTION: Common Florida, Bahamas, Caribbean.

HABITAT & BEHAVIOR: Prefer shaded areas of most marine environments, attaching to and encrusting solid substrates. Often the predominate growth in cracks, crevices, and along the walls of caves and narrow canyons. On sloping substrates, extended outer edges often overlap in a shingle-like fashion.

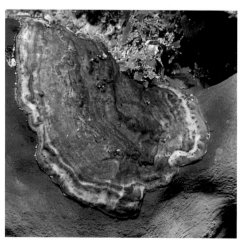

CRUSTOSE CORALLINE ALGAE

PHYLUM:
Rhodophyta
Red Algae

SIZE: Plates 1 - 18 in.
DEPTH: 0 - 130 plus ft.

**Crustose
Coralline Algae**
*Growth patterns and
color variations.*

**Crustose
Coralline Algae**
*Growth pattern and
color variation with green
Halimeda sp.*

VISUAL ID: Thin, hard, highly calcified encrusting growth taking on contours of substrate much like a painted coating. Dark red to burgundy. Outer margins may not be tightly attached.

ABUNDANCE & DISTRIBUTION: Abundant to occasional Florida, Bahamas, Caribbean.

HABITAT & BEHAVIOR: Prefer shaded areas of most marine environments, attaching to and encrusting solid substrates. Often the predominate growth in cracks, crevices, and along the walls of caves, canyons and deep drop-offs.

NOTE: Visual genus identification probable, positive identification requires laboratory examination that includes decalcification, sectioning and microscopic examination.

VISUAL ID: Several visually indistinguishable species form thin, brittle, highly calcified encrustations on surfaces of many species of algae and Turtle Grass (pictured here on Sea Pearls [pg. 219]). Surface texture generally smooth, but occasionally covered with small, knobby, cobblestone-like, reproductive structures. Usually shades of grayish lavender. Species may be classified in *Titanoderma, Fosliella,* or *Melobesia.*

ABUNDANCE & DISTRIBUTION: Abundant to occasional Florida, Bahamas, Caribbean.

HABITAT & BEHAVIOR: Common in most marine environments.

VISUAL ID: A number of species in this phylum form fuzzy masses of filaments. Generally dark red to burgundy to reddish tan. These colonies are so individually variable in appearance, and yet similar to one another, that they cannot easily be distinguished visually. Positive identification requires laboratory examination of filaments.

ABUNDANCE & DISTRIBUTION: Common Florida, Bahamas, Caribbean.

HABITAT & BEHAVIOR: Prefer sunlit areas of most marine environments. Often have no permanent holdfast and snag on branches of other plants and colonial organisms.

NOTE: Pictured specimen is possibly *Symploca hydnoides.*

BURGUNDY CRUST ALGAE
Peyssonnelia sp.
PHYLUM:
Rhodophyta
Red Algae

SIZE: 1 - 3 ft.
DEPTH: 0 - 660 ft.

LAVENDER CRUST ALGAE

PHYLUM:
Rhodophyta
Red Algae

SIZE: Diameter
$^1/_2$ - 2 in.
DEPTH: 0 - 100 ft.

FUZZ BALL ALGAE

PHYLUM:
Cyanophyta
Blue-green Algae

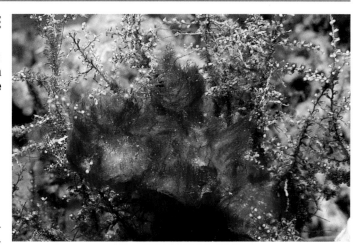

SIZE: 1 - 3 in.
DEPTH: 0 - 80 plus ft.

Coral Health and Mortality

Recognizing the signs
of coral diseases and predators

Compiled by Dr. Andrew Bruckner

Introduction

Throughout the western Atlantic, coral reefs have undergone dramatic changes as a consequence of human activity, natural disturbances, and a general deterioration of water quality. Hurricanes, disease and outbreaks of predators during the 1970s and 1980s transformed flourishing Elkhorn and Staghorn Coral thickets into fields of coral rubble or tissue-denuded skeletons. From 1983-1984, a water-borne disease wiped out more than 90 percent of the population of Caribbean's Long-spined Urchin, *Diadema antillarum*, that previously controlled algae – a major competitor of corals. This unprecedented die-off led to the widespread destruction of massive and plating corals at many sites throughout the region. However, the most significant factors leading to the degradation of coral reefs have been storms; an increase of sedimentation and nutrient run-off from land, rivers and sewage; over fishing; overgrowth by competing algae, sponges and tunicates; animal predation; bleaching; and a host of diseases.

Until the early 1990s, the only known coral diseases were White-band Disease, Black-band Disease and White Plague. The number of reported coral diseases and syndromes escalated during the mid-1990s. Today, coral diseases have now been documented to infect most common reef building corals in the Caribbean. Little is known about what causes these diseases, how a coral contracts them, and their potential long-term effects on reef systems. They may be caused by infectious pathogens, such as bacteria and fungi, stresses, elevated sea water temperatures and increased ultraviolet radiation, poor nutrition, genetic mutations (noninfectious diseases), or a combination of these and undetermined factors. Increased sedimentation, nutrients and pollutants may be responsible for an increase in pathogens or may decrease a coral's defense mechanisms and immune responses. Man's land-based activities are known to have introduced at least one coral disease, a soil fungus spread to seawater from river run-off that affects sea fans. Alarmingly, more and more reefs in unpopulated areas are being affected by diseases, despite the absence of major human impacts in these areas.

A great deal of confusion exists about the nature of coral diseases because of factors such as incomplete designation of diseases and syndromes, as well as duplication of pathogen names and their causes or agents. Most coral diseases bear names that reflect the color of the diseased or affected tissues or the pattern of tissue loss. Over 30 names have been used by the scientific community to describe coral diseases. In some cases, different names have been given to the same disease and, in other cases, signs described as a disease may, in fact, be caused by coral predators. Further complicating matters, the appearance of a disease may vary according to depth, season or geographic location and coral colonies may be infected by more than one disease simultaneously.

Through the expansion of reef monitoring programs – many involving volunteer recreational divers – and improved laboratory techniques to investigate disease development and spread, coral diseaes and predators are being more fully understood. the purpose of this review is to help define a standard to better study coral diseases and predation.

Healthy colony of Mountainous Star Coral

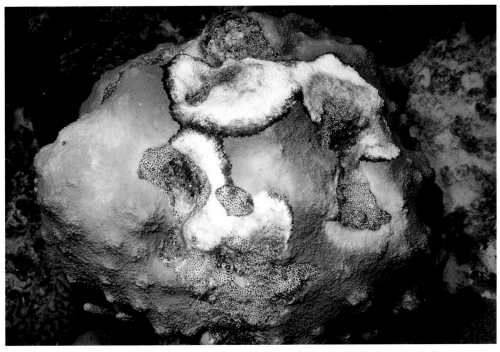

Mountainous Star Coral colony infected with Black-band Disease and Yellow-blotch Disease

Black-band Disease

VISUAL ID: Black-band Disease (BBD) is either crescent-shaped or a circular band of blackish filamentous material separating living, colored coral tissue from white, exposed skeleton. Over days to months, BBD slowly spreads in a line across a colony, killing coral tissue as it advances. Infected areas can eventually expand to six feet (two meters) across. The bands are dark maroon to black due to the photosynthetic pigments (phycocyanin and phycoerythrin) of the cyanobacteria (blue-green algae). Bands often have a white dusting of filamentous (sulfide-oxidizing) bacteria. These microorganisms consist of long, unbranched filaments (visible to the naked eye) that are intertwined to form a dense mat. This mat is loosely anchored in living tissue and is easily dislodged by water movement.

Infections normally start at the fringe of a colony, in a surface depression or at the edge of a previous injury. Once BBD is established, it advances from a fraction of an inch to an inch (2 mm to 2 cm) per day. The disease is most apparent during phases of rapid advance, which generally occur when the water is clear and calm. During a brief period of a few days after a rapid advance begins, large portions of the white skeleton is exposed before a covering of green and brown filamentous algae becomes established and spreads over the area.

CORALS AFFECTED: In the western Atlantic, 16 species of common massive and plating corals as well as several gorgonians, including sea fans and branching sea rods, have been documented with BBD to date. The Boulder Star Coral, *Montastraea annularis* complex, and Symmetrical Brain Coral, *Diploria strigosa*, sustain the majority of infections. An additional 26 coral species in the Red Sea and Indo-Pacific are also affected. Staghorn Coral, *Acropora cervicornis*, and Elkhorn Coral, *A. palmata*, have not been observed with BBD.

CAUSE: Black-band Disease is a highly infectious disease caused primarily by a cyanobacteria, *Phormidium corallyticum,* in combination with sulfide oxidizing bacteria, *Beggiatoa* spp., and sulfur reducing bacteria, *Desulfovibrio* spp. Coral tissue is killed by the hydrogen sulfide produced by these microorganisms. Other opportunistic organisms such as ciliate protozoans, flatworms, nematodes, fungal filaments, and small crustaceans are also associated with the band. Bearded Fireworms, *Hermodice carunculata*, and coral-eating snails *Coralliophila* spp. are commonly seen feeding on tissue adjacent to the bands.

ABUNDANCE & DISTRIBUTION: BBD was first discovered on the reefs of Belize and Florida in 1972, and has since been identified on the coral reefs of 26 countries. The number of corals infected with BBD on a reef fluctuates, but BBD is always present at some level, to depths of just over 100 feet. In the late summer and early fall, when water is clear and calm and temperatures reach their peak, colonies become far more susceptible to infection and the rapid spread of the disease. BBD disappears, or becomes more difficult to find, when water temperatures drop below 72 F (22 C). The disease also subsides during extended periods of low water visibility. BBD is uncommon in areas of high wave action.

IMPACT: Research has been conducted in Belize, Florida, Jamaica, Puerto Rico and the Virgin Islands to understand more about the distribution, abundance and impact of BBD. Typically, a few corals show signs of this disease on any particular reef during its active season. In a few locations up to 50 percent of coral colonies can be affected. Small colonies may be killed by BBD in weeks to months, but relatively few of the larger corals die from a single infection event. Typically, a colony loses up to half of its tissue before the disease disappears. Unfortunately, colonies are occasionally reinfected. Partial tissue loss affects a coral's ability to reproduce. Also, the portion of a coral killed is often colonized by organisms such as boring sponges that erode the skeleton, further limiting the colony's ability to recover.

Symmetrical Brain Coral infected with Black-band Disease. [right]

Spread of Black-band Disease over two week period. [middle]

Blushing Star Coral infected with Black-band Disease. [bottom left]

Bearded Fireworm feeding on coral tissue adjacent to diseased band. [bottom right]

White-band Disease

VISUAL ID: Typically White-band Disease (WBD), which affects branching corals, starts at the base of a colony and progresses toward branch tips, but occasionally it begins in the middle of a colony, especially at the points where branches begin. Unlike BBD, there is no obvious black mat; instead, colonies affected by WBD display a margin of slowly advancing tissue decay, which exposes a contrasting bright white area of limestone skeleton next to dying tissue. The disease causes tissue to peel away form the skeleton at a fairly uniform rate of just under a quarter inch (5 mm) per day, although the disease can advance much more rapidly. The exposed skeleton, varying from a fraction of an inch to four inches wide (a few millimeters to 10 cm) is colonized by algae in a matter of days. An entire colony rarely suffers complete mortality; however, recovered colonies are often reinfected.

CORALS AFFECTED: Staghorn Coral, *Acropora cervicornis,* Elkhorn Coral, *A. palmata,* and Fused Staghorn Coral, *A. prolifera.*

CAUSE: No definitive cause has been identified for WBD; however, a host of bacteria, fungi and protozoans are often found at the site of infection. Rod-shaped, bacteria-like organisms have been identified within the coral tissue of some infected colonies, but these also occur in corals that appear healthy.

ABUNDANCE & DISTRIBUTION: WBD was first observed in 1977 on reefs surrounding St. Croix, USVI. It has since been identified throughout the wider Caribbean and in Red Sea, Indo-Pacific, and the Gulf of Oman. Although WBD only affects acroporids on Caribbean reefs, the same, or a similar disease, has been observed on several other genera in the Indo-Pacific. The signs of WBD are similar to White Plague, a disease that affects Caribbean corals other than Staghorn Coral and Elkhorn Coral. In the Caribbean, the incidence of WBD ranges from less than one percent to 64 percent of the colonies in a single area. WBD epizootics (the equivalent of an epidemic in humans) were first reported throughout the Caribbean in the late 1970s and again in 1980s and 1990s. The disease is still common today; however, it may be less conspicuous because of a marked decline of the three species of *Acropora* and because of confusion with a similar disease that also affects the same coral species (see below).

IMPACT: White-band disease is believed to be the major factor responsible for the rapid loss of Caribbean acroporid corals. Mass mortalities have led to a virtual elimination of Staghorn and Elkhorn thickets from shallow reef environments throughout the region. For example, large stands of Elkhorn Coral that were formerly abundant in the USVI (St. Croix) declined from 85 percent cover to 5 percent within 10 years. White-band disease is the only coral disease to date that has been documented to cause major changes in the composition and structure of reefs.

Related White Syndromes

VISUAL ID: A second form of White-band Disease, known as White-band Disease Type II, was first identified in the Bahamas in 1993. WBD II is believed to be more virulent, causing tissue death at a much more rapid rate. The disease spreads from the base of a colony toward the branch tips. It appears as a band of bleached tissue varying from just less than one inch to eight inches (2 to 20 cm) wide that separates the normal pigmented tissue from the white dead skeleton. A bacteria of the genus *Vibrio,* which lives on the surface mucus of the bleached tissue, may cause WBD II.

White Pox (POX) and **Patchy Necrosis** (PN) also affect Elkhorn Coral. These diseases are easily distinguished from WBD. Both diseases appear as small patches of dead tissue that are surrounded completely by normal tissue in contrast to the prominent bands of tissue decay associated with WBD. Patches are most frequently located on the upper surfaces of branches.

White Pox was first reported in the Florida Keys during 1996, but is now believed to occur throughout the Caribbean. POX starts as small, circular white spots or patches on the upper or lower surfaces of the branches. The numerous white patches are bare of coral tissue. Once infected, the patches expand rapidly and are presumed to eventually cause a colony's death.

Patchy Necrosis has been observed on Elkhorn colonies throughout the Caribbean since 1994 but, unlike POX, it rarely kills an entire colony. The disease typically appears on the upper surfaces of Elkhorn Coral branches as one or more irregular patches of denuded skeleton, ranging from less than an inch to four inches (2 to 10 cm) in diameter. When first infected patches increase rapidly; however, the spread slows markedly after a few days and eventually stops. Typically, corals afflicted with PN lose relatively small patches of tissue. As with other diseases, colonies may be reinfected in new locations. After several infectious events, Elkhorn branches are a mosaic of live tissue interspersed with white, recently killed areas and older lesions colonized by turf algae. These areas eventually heal over.

It is possible that POX and PN are the same diseases that were observed to affect corals differently in the locations from where they were described.

Staghorn Coral infected with White-band Disease. [middle left] *Elkhorn Coral infected with White-band Disease.* [middle right] *Detail of White Pox on Elkhorn Coral.* [bottom left] *Elkhorn Coral infected with Patchy Necrosis.* [bottom right]

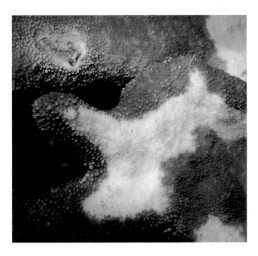

White Plague

VISUAL ID: White Plague (WP), which is similar in appearance to White-band Disease, affects massive and plating corals. Tissue loss begins at the base or margin of a colony, or next to a previously diseased area, and quickly spreads. A sharp line separates healthy tissue from the bare skeleton; however there is no visible mat of organisms at the disease front. A fine, but distinct, narrow band of bleached tissue may separate normal, fully pigmented tissue from the white, exposed skeleton. Tissue loss progresses up to $^3/_4$ of an inch (2 cm) per day.

Two forms of White Plague have been described: Plague Type I, which was documented in the 1970s and 1980s, and Plague Type II first reported in the mid-1990s from the same reefs in Florida. The disease signs of both forms are similar, and there is some overlap of affected species. However, in White Plague Type II the disease spreads rapidly, with the ability to kill a small coral in just one to two days; White Plague Type I advances only a few millimeters each day and can take from 3 to 4 months to kill an entire colony. Elliptical Star Coral, *Dichocoenia stokesi,* a species never observed with WP in the 1970s or 1980s, appears particularly vulnerable to White Plague Type II.

CORALS AFFECTED: At least 17 species of massive and plating corals, primarily Starlet Corals, *Siderastera* spp., Cactus Corals, *Mycetophyllia* spp., and Boulder Brain Coral, *Colpophyllia natans.* It does not affect Staghorn Coral, *Acropora cervicornis* or Elkhorn Coral, *A. palmata.*

CAUSE: White Plague Type II is caused by a rod-shaped bacterium in the genus *Sphingomonas.* Several bacteria were found to live in association with White Plague Type I, but have never been confirmed as the cause of the disease.

ABUNDANCE & DISTRIBUTION: WP was first described from the Florida Keys in 1977 on Starlet Coral, Cactus Coral and Boulder Brain Coral. In the 1980s it was also observed on Mountainous Star Coral, *Montastraea faveolata.* Outbreaks have been reported from Puerto Rico and the USVI, and many other locations. Plague Type II emerged during 1995 in the Florida Keys, initially attacking the Elliptical Star Coral, *Dichocoenia stokesi,* a coral previously presumed to be resistant to diseases. Due to the rapid advance of this disease, small corals are killed within a few days. Outbreaks of white plague among large colonies of mountainous star corals and brain corals were reported from around the Caribbean in the spring and summer of 2001, with colonies moe than a meter in diameter being killed in about a week.

IMPACT: In an extensive study conducted in the Florida Keys in the 1970s, involving nearly 10,000 coral colonies, up to 73 percent on some were found to be infected with Plague Type I. Plague Type II spread throughout the Florida Keys between 1995 and 1998, with the highest number of infections on Elliptical Star Corals (up to 38 percent were affected on some reefs), many of which died within days of becoming infected. Nearly half of the brain corals on one reef in Puerto Rico were affected in 1996; fortunately most suffered only partial mortality and the disease has since declined in abundance.

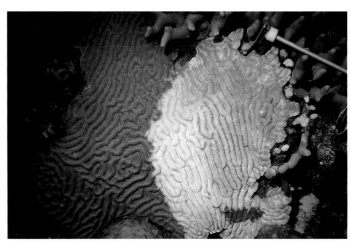

Boulder Brain Coral infected with White Plague Type I. The disease can kill an entire colony in two to three months.

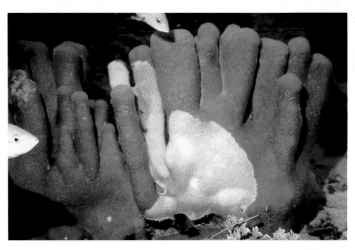

Pillar Coral infected with White Plague Type II. The disease spreads very rapidly and can kill an entire small colony in one to two days!

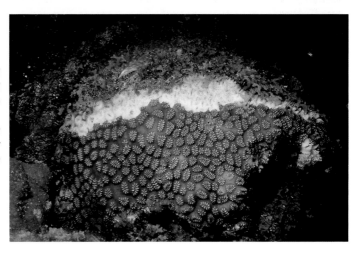

Elliptical Star Coral was never observed with White Plague in the 1970s or 1980s, but now appears to be particularly vulnerable to White Plague Type II.

Yellow-blotch Disease

VISUAL ID: Yellow-blotch Disease (YBD) begins as a pale yellow, circular blotch of tissue in the middle of a colony or as a narrow band at the edge of a colony. Infected areas are surrounded by normal, dark green to brown tissue. Affected tissue is translucent, but still contains a reduced number of symbiotic algae (zooxanthellae). As the pale yellow leading edge of YBD advances, tissue adjacent to the exposed skeleton gradually darkens and dies. The band advances up to $\frac{3}{8}$ of an inch (1 cm) per month. Because the spread is relatively slow, colonies rarely have a prominent area of white, exposed skeleton. Typically, tissue mortality is restricted to small one- to four-square-inch (5-10 cm) irregular blotches. Although the rate of tissue loss is much slower than other coral diseases, an infection can exist for years, eventually killing large colonies.

CORALS AFFECTED: Boulder Star Corals, *Montastraea annularis* complex, are most frequently affected, but also reported on Cavernous Star Coral, *M. cavernosa,* and Boulder Brain Coral *Colpophyllia natans.*

CAUSE: An unusual crystalline material has been observed inside infected polyps, but the origin of this material is unknown. This condition has been confused with bleaching and has been incorrectly referred to as "Ring Bleaching". Because of its appearance in advanced stages, it is occasionally referred to as "Yellow-band Disease".

ABUNDANCE & DISTRIBUTION: Yellow-blotch Disease was first identified in 1994 in the lower Florida Keys, and has since been reported from Curacao, Bonaire, Panama, Mexico and Puerto Rico.

IMPACT: Monitoring efforts for YBD in the Caribbean have recorded an increased incidence, accompanied by alarming coral mortality in the late 1990s. The disease kills coral tissue at a rate of 3 to 6 inches (7-15 cm) per year, which is considerably slower than the rate observed for other diseases. However, corals become infected in many locations and infections persist for several years. YBD appears to be particularly common on the largest and oldest corals found on a reef. In a specific area, up to 50 percent of boulder-type corals may be infected.

Yellow-blotch Disease starts as a pale yellow to white blotch [below] *or band* [below right].

As the disease advances the tissue behind the narrow pale blotch or band darkens to a yellowish brown and eventually dies.

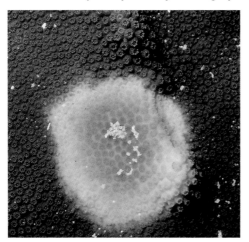

Yellow-blotch Disease infected
Great Star Coral [right],
Boulder Star Coral [below middle left]
Symmetrical Brain Coral [below middle right]

Yellow-blotch Disease spreads
much slower than other coral diseases,
but none-the-less will eventually kill
an entire colony.
Mountainous Star Coral colony
in August 1999 [botom left]
and the same colony
May 2001. [bottom right]

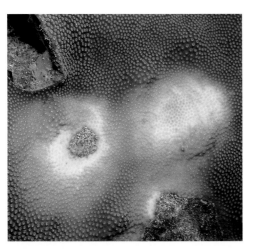

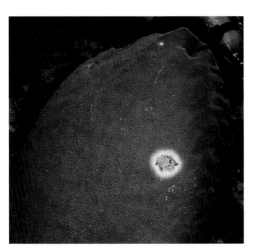

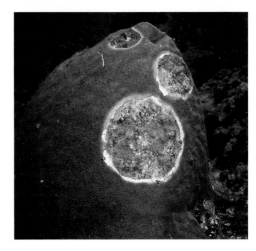

Red-band Disease

VISUAL ID: Red-band Disease (RBD) consists of a narrow band or line of filamentous cyanobacteria (blue-green algae) that advances slowly across the surface of a coral killing living tissue as it advances. There are two types of RBD, referred to as RBD-1 and RBD-2.

RBD-1, like Black-band Disease, forms a distinct band that separates living coral tissue from bare white skeleton as it advances a few millimeters each day. Unlike BBD, the band is red to maroon and the cyanobacterial filaments are often more loosely organized and less mat-like.

RBD-2 is visibly different from RBD-1. During daylight, the filaments spread like a net over a colony's surface. At night the band forms a compact "balled-up" mat at the interface between the living tissue and the exposed skeleton.

CORALS AFFECTED: RBD-1 infects Lettuce Corals, *Agaricia* spp., Boulder Brain Coral, *Colpophyllia natans*, Cactus Corals, *Mycetophyllia* spp., Blushing Star Coral, *Stephanocoenia intersepta*, and the Common Seafan, *Gorgonia ventalina*.

RBD-2 infects Symmetrical Brain Coral, *Diploria strigosa*, the Boulder Star Corals, *Montastraea annularis* complex, Great Star Coral, *M. cavernosa*, Mustard Hill Coral, *Porites astreoides*, and Massive Starlet Coral, *Siderastrea radians*.

CAUSE: Based on the structure of microscopic filaments from Belize, RBD appears to be caused by at least two species of cyanobacteria: *Schithothrix* and *Spirulina*. However, an examination of the genetic structure of RBD-1 cyanobacteria (using 16s RNA) indicates that they may be more closely related to other cyanobacteria (*Oscillatoria* and the *Gloeotheca-Gloecapsa*). Two species of *Oscillatoria* were observed in RBD-2 samples from the Bahamas.

ABUNDANCE AND DISTRIBUTION: RBD-1 was first observed on sea fans during 1983 in Belize. RBD has also been observed in the Bahamas, Curacao, Puerto Rico and Jamaica. RBD-2 was first reported in the early 1990s in the Bahamas. No information is available on the abundance or impact of RBD.

Common Sea Fan infected with Red-band Disease Type 1.

Cactus Coral infected with Red-band Disease Type 1. The disease closely resembles Black-band Disease, but is red to maroon, rather than black to dark maroon, and is also generally more filamentous.

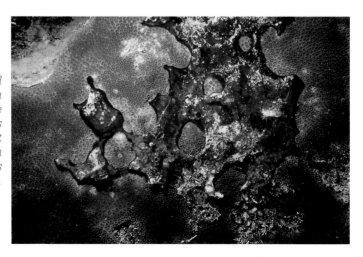

Lettuce Coral infected with Red-band Disease Type 1; note the filamentous band.

Boulder Star Coral infected with Red-band Disease Type 2. The filaments spread out like a net in a diffuse fashion over the colony's surface.

Dark-spot Disease

VISUAL ID: Dark-spot Disease (DSD) appears as circular to irregular areas of pale discolored tissue with darkened polyps or spots in the middle of normal tissue, or at the colony's margin. Discolored tissue spreads as the affected tissue dies. On Massive Starlet Coral discolored areas may be pink, brown, or blue, although colonies with a bluish hue may be showing signs of bleaching. In a few instances, most noticeably on Blushing Star Coral, the darkened polyps are slightly depressed and smaller than normal polyps.

CORALS AFFECTED: DSD is most commonly observed on Massive Starlet Coral, *Siderastrea siderea,* and Blushing Star Coral, *Stephanocoenia intersepta,* but has also been reported on Boulder Star Corals, *Montastraea annularis* complex.

CAUSE: The cause of DSD is unknown

ABUNDANCE & DISTRIBUTION: First reported from Colombia during the late 1990s. This condition now occurs on reefs throughout the Caribbean, but little information is available on its abundance or impact.

Irregular Growths:
Hyperplasm and Neoplasm (Tumors)

VISUAL ID: A hyperplasm is an area of accelerated growth of coral polyps. It results in corallite distortion and other malformations. Ridges and valleys on brain corals, or circular polyps in star corals are enlarged and project above the colony surface. Polyps are visible but appear exaggerated.

A neoplasm is an irregular, calcified mass of skeleton that projects above the surface of the colony. It is covered with undifferentiated tissue that lacks symbiotic algae and the structural organization of normal tissue that makes individual polyps unrecognizable. Certain cells within the neoplasm (calicoblastic epithelial cells) grow and multiply at a rapid rate causing a progressive increase in the size of the tumor. This condition may slowly advance upward and outward as tissue in the center of the tumor dies.

CORALS AFFECTED: All corals are believed to be susceptible to both types. Neoplasm generally affects Elkhorn Coral, *Acropora palmata.*

CAUSE: Some tumors may form in response to algal and fungal agents, or certain stresses such as high ultraviolet radiation, while others may be genetic mutations.

ABUNDANCE & DISTRIBUTION: Abnormal/irregular growths on corals were first reported over 30 years ago. These conditions appear to be widespread, but their abundance and impact are unknown.

Blushing Star Coral infected with Dark-spot Disease. Note the pale discolored tissue; there is also an area of Black-band Disease near the colony's center. [right]

When Massive Starlet Coral is infected with Dark-spot Disease the tissue often has splotches of reddish pink. [bottom right]

Elkhorn Coral infected with Neoplasm Tumor. [bottom left]

Boulder Brain Coral infected with Hyperplasm tumors. [opposite page left]

Mountainous Star Coral infected with Hyperplasm tumors. [opposite page right]

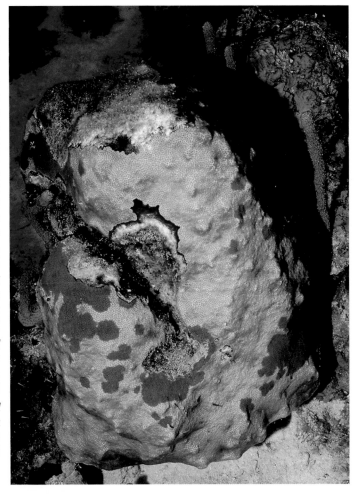

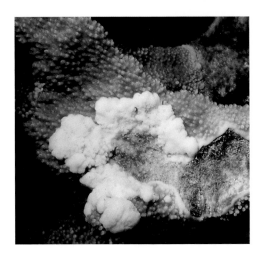

Coral Bleaching

VISUAL ID: Bleaching results in the loss of the symbiotic algae (zooxanthellae) contained within coral tissue, or as a reduction of the photosynthetic pigments of the zooxanthellae that give the coral its normal color. In either case, the coral appears lighter in color, mottled or white. In some species, such as Massive Starlet Coral, *Siderastrea siderea,* partially bleached colonies may be a shade of blue or pink.

CORALS AFFECTED: Apparently all species are susceptible.

CAUSE: Bleaching may be caused by a wide range of environmental stresses, but is most commonly caused by elevated water temperatures and increased ultraviolet radiation from prolonged periods of clear water and flat seas. Corals also bleach when exposed to extremes in salinity, pollution, increased sedimentation, or unusually low temperatures. In a few cases, bacteria and protozoans have been known to cause bleaching.

ABUNDANCE & DISTRIBUTION: Coral bleaching of single corals has been observed on coral reefs for over 100 years, but only recently have mass bleaching events been recorded. Most coral bleaching events are extremely localized with only certain colonies on a particular reef affected. The intensity of bleaching, number of species affected, distribution of bleached corals, and amount of mortality caused by bleaching has varied considerably among reefs and years. However, bleaching events appear to have increased in intensity, frequency and geographic distribution in the past two decades. Six major episodes of bleaching have occurred since 1979, with the most severe in 1998.

IMPACT: Without symbiotic algae, which provide corals with their major source of energy, bleached corals are under increased stress. In most circumstances, corals recover fully from bleaching, but recovery takes several months with some colonies experiencing partial tissue loss. If stresses are prolonged, most, if not all, of a coral's polyps die. It is widely believed that bleached corals become more susceptible to coral diseases.

Bleaching does not affect all colonies, even of the same species, uniformly. Side by side bleached and not bleached colonies of Maze Coral.

Bleaching colony of Yellow Pencil Coral.

Massive bleaching event of sheet corals on wall in Bonaire in 1998. [right]

Severely bleached colony of White Star Sheet Coral. [bottom left]

Under some circumstances, corals can recover from bleaching. Same colony fully recovered several months later. [bottom right]

However, if the stresses that caused bleaching are prolonged, most if not all of the coral polyps die.

Gorgonian Diseases

VISUAL ID: Reports of disease on octocorals have increased in recent years. At least three diseases are now known to affect Caribbean sea fans, *Gorgonia* spp. Black-band Disease (BBD) and Red-band Disease (RBD) were first observed in 1982, while a third disease, Aspergillosis, was reported in 1996. Octocorals are also affected by tumors and various invertebrate predators, and may also be overgrown by fire corals, *Millepora* spp.

BBD affects sea fans and the sea plumes *Psuedoterigorgia* spp. while RBD has only been observed on sea fans. Both RBD and BBD start at the base of a colony, or within the blade at sites of previous injuries. The disease forms a characteristic band, 1-20 mm wide that progressively advances outward as it kills sea fan tissue. Once the tissue is dead, the skeleton quickly becomes fouled with sediment and algae.

Aspergillosis caused by a soil fungus, *Aspergillus* spp. results in the death of tissue and erosion of the skeleton. Common Sea Fan, *Gorgonia ventalina,* and the Venus Sea Fan, *G. flabellum,* display one or more irregular patches that lack living tissue. These areas expand in size until they eventually result in holes in the blades. The living tissue surrounding these lesions often becomes dark purple and may develop spherical nodules or galls (tumors). Many sea fans often have similar-appearing lesions, dark areas and tumors that have no association with Aspergillosis. The disease can only be verified by the presence of fine white fungal filaments adjacent to living tissue, that is extremely difficult to detect in the field with the naked eye.

Sea fans are commonly observed with dark purple, round or oblong growths or nodules (tumors) on the main branches or on the blade. These tumors can increase in size and number and spread over a colony, and may result in tissue death and erosion of the skeleton.

Sea fans commonly have tumors that appear as dark purple, round or oblong nodules that with growth may result in tissue death and erosion of the fan's skeleton.

Sea Fan infected with Red-band Disease. The infection usually starts at the bottom of the colony and spreads upward eventually killing the entire colony.

Aspergillosis is a fungus infection attacking sea fans. The infection kills patches of tissue, ultimately causing holes in the fan.

Branching Fire Coral often overgrows sea fans and other gorgonians.

Gorgonian Predators

Several species of snails feed on gorgonians including Flamingo Tongue, *Cyphoma gibbosum*, Fingerprint Cyphoma, *C. signatum*, Spotted Cyphoma, *C. macgintyi*, and Short Coral Snail, *Coralliophila caribaea*. These snails typically graze a trail across the gorgonian as they consume tissue. Grazing trails occasionally expose the spicules (skeletal elements in the colony's structure) in a line the width of the predators' bodies. The other coral-eating snails, *Coralliophila* spp., typically remain close to the holdfast and are more difficult to detect. They often feed in small clusters on a sea fan or sea plume leaving characteristic feeding scars that extend up the blade in narrow lines. The Bearded Fireworm, *Hermodice carunculata*, is also a common gorgonian predator commonly feeding on Deep Water Sea Fans, *Iciligorgia schrammi*, and other gorgonians.

Bearded Fireworms commonly feed on Deep Water Sea Fans and other gorgonians. [right]

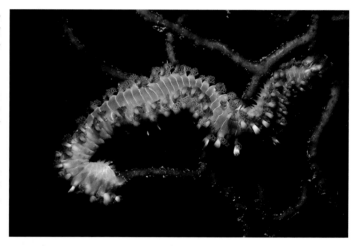

Detail of gorgonian tissue damage from feeding Flamingo Tongue. [below left]

Spotted Cyphomas commonly feed on Regal Sea Fans and other gorgonians. [below right]

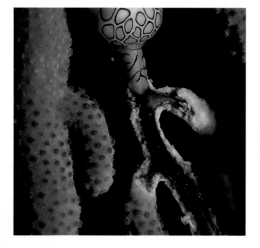

*An infestation of adult and juvenile
Flamingo Tongues ravages a bushy gorgonian.* [top]

A pair of adult Fingerprint Cyphomas feed on a sea rod. [below right]
*Juvenile Fingerprint Cyphoma
feeds on Deep Water Sea Fan.* [below left]

Coral Predation

Predation of stony corals by coral eating animals (corallivores) is much less prevalent in the Caribbean than in the Indo-Pacific. The dominant Caribbean corallivores include the Green Clinging Crab, *Mithrax sculptus,* a copepod, coral snails, *Coralliophila* spp., and Top Shells, *Calliostoma* spp., the Bearded Fireworm, *Hermodice carunculata,* and a few fishes. Certain butterflyfishes (Chaetodontidae), damselfishes (Pomacentridae) and parrotfishes (Scaridae) occasionally browse on coral polyps. Only the Stoplight Parrotfish, *Sparisoma viride,* consumes large amounts of living coral tissue, primarily star corals and Boulder Brain Coral, *Colpophyllia natans.* With the exception of fireworms and the coral snails, both of which can cause conspicuous damage, the majority of invertebrates cause little obvious damage to their host. The only known large-scale coral mortality associated with invertebrate predation occurred in Jamaica, when Staghorn Coral, *Acropora cervicornis,* failed to recover after corallivores concentrated on the few remaining living colonies and fragments following hurricane destruction.

Parrotfish Focused Biting

VISUAL ID: Several parrotfish, including the Queen, *Scarus vetula,* Stoplight, *Sparisoma viride,* and Rainbow, *Scarus guacamaia* frequently feed on live coral. These fish typically take numerous small bites, called "Spot Biting," over the surface of coral heads creating obvious paired grazing scars. Large female and male Stoplight Parrotfish often return repeatedly to bite the same area of a coral head, producing large obvious lesions on the colony's surface. These lesions spread progressively across the coral, but rarely kill an entire colony completely. This behavior, called Focused Biting, has been incorrectly referred to as "Rapid Wasting Disease". Signs of fish predation are distinct from signs of disease. Damage caused by fish bites generally removes both living tissue and the top layers of the skeleton, whereas disease leaves the coral skeleton intact.

Focused biting caused by Stoplight Parrotfishes is observed most frequently on Lobed Star Coral, *Montastraea annularis,* Mountainous Star Coral, *M. faveolata,* and Boulder Brain Coral, *Colpophyllia natans,* although most stony corals are occasionally bitten as well. Affected colonies appear to have been physically abraded, with damage extending in one- to four-inch (2 to 10 cm) wide strips. Fish characteristically remove tissue and skeleton from the top portions of a single lobe of star corals, before beginning the same behavior on an adjacent, previously undamaged lobe. The process is repeated for days to weeks until multiple lobes on an individual colony are damaged. Parrotfish bite at prominent knobs or projections on Mountainous Star Coral leaving golf ball-sized, or larger, lesions. Boulder Brain Coral grazing usually begins at the colony's edge and methodically progresses forming a uniform strip. Plating- and branching-type corals are usually bitten around their edges and branch tips. An extensive release of coral mucus is often associated with recent bite marks.

ABUNDANCE & DISTRIBUTION: Parrotfish predation on coral was first reported over 100 years ago. It can be observed on practically every reef and affects most coral species in the Caribbean.

IMPACT: Boulder Brain Coral is occasionally killed by parrotfish grazing; however, most stony coral species slowly heal from fish bite injuries.

Parrotfish bites of living coral completely remove the living tissue and upper layers of limestone skeleton, easily distinguishing them from diseased tissue. Damaged Boulder Brain Coral colony. [right]
Damaged Lobed Star Coral colony. [far right]

A terminal phase Stoplight Parrotfish takes a focused bite from a living Lobed Star Coral colony. There is also evidence of repeated biting on adjacent lobes. [right]

Parrotfish grazing scars from "Spot Biting" on Star Coral. [below center left]

Initial phase Stoplight Parrotfish feeds on Lobed Star Coral. [below center right]

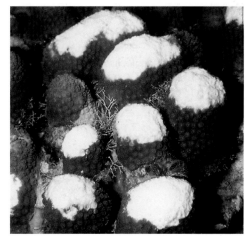

261

Bearded Fireworm Predation
Hermodice carunculata

VISUAL ID: Bearded Fireworms prey on most species of corals, but appear to have a preference for branching corals and corals that have been weakened by disease. They feed primarily on branch tips of Staghorn Coral, *Acropora cervicornis.* Damage caused by worms is very conspicuous, but feeding behavior may not be observed as worms primarily feed at night. Bearded Fireworm damage can be differentiated from disease by its location near branch tips; diseases affecting this species generally spread from the base toward branch tips.

Short Coral Snail
Coralliophila abbreviata

VISUAL ID: The Short Coral Snail, *Coralliophila abbreviata,* is found on over 20 species of stony corals and occasionally on soft corals. Small aggregations of up to 20 snails regularly cluster together. The snails are rarely noticed because of a camouflage of algal growth. Smaller snails tend to live at the base of the colony, or under flattened plates near the periphery of dead tissue. They emerge to feed at night. Larger snails will aggregate in the open on branches of Elkhorn Coral, and occasionally on other species, where they create prominent grazing scars.

CORALS AFFECTED: Elkhorn Coral, *Acropora palmata,* Staghorn Coral, *A. cervicornis,* Massive Starlet Coral, *Siderastrea siderea* and Lettuce Coral, *Agaricia agaricites,* but snails are most common on Lobed Star Coral, *Montastraea annularis* where hundreds of animals may gather between the lobes. Snail predation may be confused with White Syndromes, but can be easily distinguished by its scalloped pattern matching the shape and size of the predatory snails.

ABUNDANCE & DISTRIBUTION: In Florida and Puerto Rico, large snails are unusually common on Elkhorn Coral possibly because corals are scarcer and populations of the Caribbean Spiny Lobster, *Panulirus argus,* their historic predators, have been overharvested.

IMPACT: In general, corals sustain small amounts of predation by snails, especially the branching corals that grow at relatively fast rates. However, because these snails can aggregate in large numbers and can grow quite large (up to about 2 inches [5 cm] in length), they occasionally kill entire colonies.

Bearded Fireworm feeds on Orange Cup Coral.

Bearded Fireworm feeds on Staghorn Coral; note living tissue has been stripped from branch tip. [left]

The shells of Short Coral Snails are well camouflaged with algal growth; note five are in the picture. [far left]

Short Coral Snails clustered near the base of Elkhorn Coral colony. [left]

Damselfish Predation

VISUAL ID: Damselfishes, primarily the Threespot, *Stegastes planifrons,* are aggressive, territorial fishes that create algal gardens which they vigorously defended from other herbivores. They typically take numerous small bites over the surface of the coral colony killing an area of living polyps that is colonized by tufts of algae. [right] These injuries have been misidentified as an infection and inappropriately called "White-spot Disease."

Staghorn Coral, *Acropora cervicornis,* and Elkhorn Coral, *A. palmata,* colonies will attempt to grow over the injury, but the damselfish will continue to bite at the same spot causing the production of a chimney-like structure with an algal tuft growing on the end. [far right] Typically, the fish removes many polyps forming numerous chimneys on a single colony. If the damselfish leaves the area, coral tissue will eventually cover the injury creating what appears to be a spire extending from the branch's surface.

Damselfishes tend to damage the projecting ridges of brain corals. As algae colonize the ridges, the fish continue to remove adjacent tissue causing a progressive spread of the algal patch [middle left]. These injuries have also been misidentified as a disease called "Ridge Mortality."

ABUNDANCE & DISTRIBUTION: Damselfish predation occurs throughout the region.

IMPACT: Continued tissue removal by Damselfish can eventually kill an entire colony.

Sponge and Tunicate Overgrowth

Overgrowth and encrustation by organisms competing for space with corals, such as sponges, algae and tunicates, may eventually cause the death of stony corals and gorgonians. Most sponges associated with coral overgrowth first colonize dead areas at the margins of living tissue, or substrate adjacent to colonies. However, some sponge species bore directly into a coral's skeleton by secreting tiny amounts of acid, which riddle the structure with chambers. This damage may compromise the structure to a point where sections break away from the colony. Other competitive sponges and tunicates infiltrate corals by injecting compounds that kill the living tissue of stony corals.

In recent years, the occurrence of overgrowths appears to have increased at many locations around the Caribbean. This growing problem may be the result of excess nutrients, bacteria and suspended particles carried into the sea by runoff stimulating the growth of plankton and, in turn, providing additional food for sponges and tunicates.

Sponges

Most sponges that are associated with corals first colonize exposed skeletal areas that lack living tissue, or the reef substrate adjacent to a coral. They invade a colony from its edge, or from an area that died in the past. The Yellow Boring Sponge [next] is unusual, in that its larvae settle on the coral's living surface, kill a portion to expose the underlying skeleton, and then bore into its tissue.

Yellow Boring Sponge, *Siphonodictyon coralliphagum,* varies from bright sulfur-yellow to lemon-yellow [bottom left], orange [middle right] and white [bottom right]. The larvae of this species settle directly on mound-building and brain corals and kill the tissue, which provides a portal into the underlying skeleton. In most cases, the majority of the sponge lives within the internal skeleton of the coral with only its excurrent openings (oscula) extending above the surface; however, on occasion large areas of the sponge are visible [bottom left].

Coral Overgrowth

Species in genus *Cliona*, which are discussed next, include several species of encrusting sponges that attack and erode the surface of living corals. These sponges kill the living tissue, excavate the upper layers of the coral skeleton, and create a series of cavities and tunnels within the colonies. Members of the genus secrete acid from specialized cells that dissolves, etches and chips away at the coral skeleton and then expel tiny fragments of limestone through the excurrent openings. Because clionid sponges appear to increase in number and size in areas with high concentrations of organic matter and bacteria, their presence may serve in the future as an indicator of pollution.

Red Boring Sponge, *Cliona delitrix,* is bright red-orange. Although the species appears to encrust a coral colony's surface, it actually bores into the limestone skeleton [far right}. Numerous low wart-like spots containing tiny incurrent pores cover the surfaces. Scattered excurrent openings with large fleshy, flexible lips protrude prominently. The sponge attacks mound-building corals and will kill an entire coral colony within several years. Sponge Zoanthid, *Parazoanthus parasiticus,* and Sponge Brittle Star, *Ophiothrix suensonii,* often live on the surface of this species [right].

Coral Encrusting Sponge is a complex of identically appearing sponges, *Cliona langae, C. aprica* and *C. caribea,* that can only be distinguished to species by microscopic examination of their structural spicules. The characteristic brown to olive-brown color is derived from symbiotic algae living within their tissue. Numerous, tiny, pore-like excurrent openings cover their smooth surfaces. The sponges rapidly encrust the surfaces of dead coral occasionally covering large portions of a reef's substrate. They later spread over nearly any species of living coral encountered eroding the colonies' to a depth of one half to three quarters of an inch (1 – 2 cm) [right]. A narrow white band of exposed skeleton often separates living coral polyps from the sponge [far right]. Coral polyps bordering the invasion appear undisturbed. The sponge spreads approximately a quarter of an inch (1 cm) a month.

Brown Variable Sponge, *Anthosigmella varians,* forms a soft, thin tan to olive-brown carpet with raised, volcano-shaped excurrent openings that occasionally have irregular raised structures scattered over the surface. These encrustations may be several yards wide. The skeletal features of overgrown corals are often visible beneath the encrustation, but can be distinguished easily by the presence of excurrent openings [right]. The invader kills coral colonies as it spreads [far right]. At least 12 species of corals are known to be affected by Brown Variable Sponge.

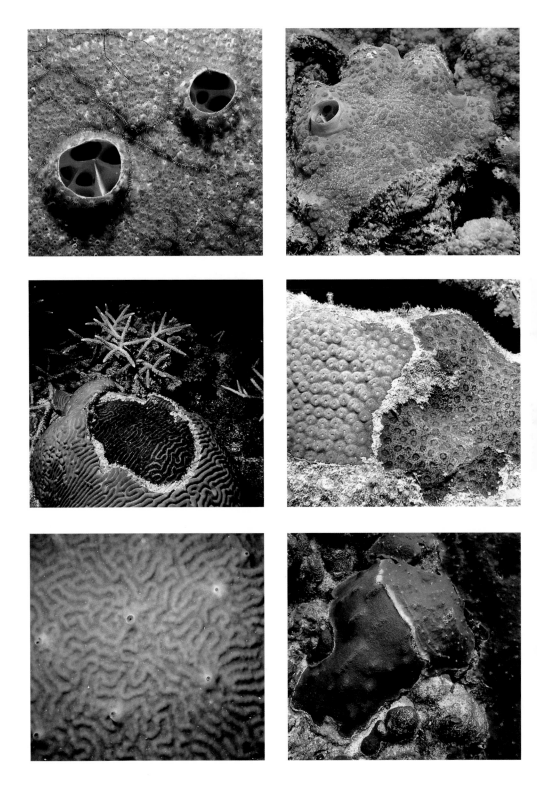

Puffy Overgrowing Sponge, *Chondrilla nucula,* is shades of brown with small scattered excurrent openings that protrude above the sponge's surface. Colonies begin on a dead area before spreading over a coral colony's surface killing living tissue as they spread [far right]. The coral's skeletal features are often visible through the encrustation, but the sponge can be differentiated from living coral by its excurrent openings [right].

Not all encrusting-type sponges overgrow or bioerode living corals. For example, Orange Icing Sponge, *Mycale laevis,* frequently seen underneath the surface of plating corals, actually protects the colony from invading invertebrates.

Cnidarians

Branching Fire Coral, *Millepora alcicornis,* and **Blade Fire Coral,** *Millepora complanata,* grow in erect colonies in areas with surge or currents. On occasion, both species overgrow and encrust neighboring stony corals and gorgonians eventually killing the colonies.

Encrusting Gorgonian, *Erythropodium caribaeorum,* forms a thin mat that often encrusts an area several feet wide. When the polyps' long tentacles are extended, the colony appears fuzzy; when contracted, it has the appearance of smooth brown leather. Colonies usually encrust the sides of reef substrate, but will also overgrow and kill living stony corals.

Encrusting Gorgonian overgrowing colony of Boulder Star Coral.

Encrusting Gorgonian overgrows colony of Massive Starlet Coral.

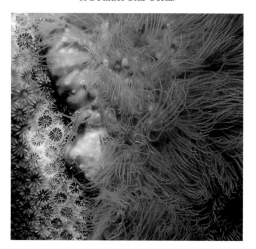

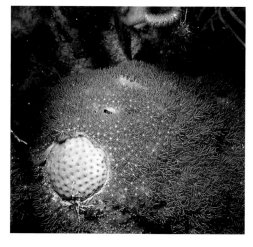

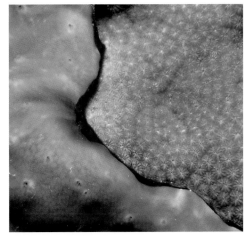

Blade Fire Coral overgrowing colony of Mountainous Star Coral.

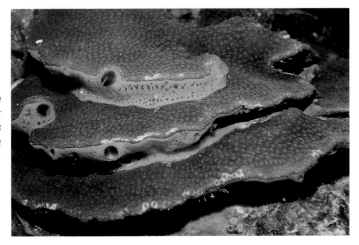

Orange Icing Sponge often encrusts the under surface of plating corals protecting them from bioerosion.

Tunicates

Overgrowing Mat Tunicate, *Trididemnum solidum,* grows in colonies of tiny tunicates embedded in a tough, smooth leathery tunic, which resembles a coating of blue-green or lime-green candle wax. The surface is covered with numerous, pore-like incurrent siphons interspersed with a scattering of larger communal excurrent siphons. Colonies encrust large areas of a reef and will overgrow and kill most species of stony corals. Overgrowing Mat Tunicates often go through periods of rapid growth before dying back, and occasionally disappear completely from an affected area leaving behind exposed substrate. Peeling a colony off a coral is thought to cause further spread of the organism.

Overgrowing Mat Tunicate covers colony of Boulder Star Coral.

Solutions

Coral diseases have probably been around for as long as there have been reefs; however, they are believed to have proliferated with direct pressure from an ever-growing human population. Coral diseases as indicators of environmental deterioration have prompted growing attention from the media, government, non-government agencies, environmental organizations and scientists. It remains unclear whether the recent increase in the number and severity of diseases is a natural short-term event or human-induced degradation with serious long-term ramifications. However, it has been documented that coral diseases, at their current levels, often cause coral mortality at rates that greatly exceed the growth of the fastest growing corals. Colonies that are hundreds of years old can be killed by disease in a matter of months, and these corals cannot be replaced in our lifetime.

In many parts of the Caribbean, losses of live coral may be occurring because reef communities are out of balance. With the dramatic loss of apex predators such as groupers, snappers, barracuda, and other key organisms such as lobsters and octopuses to overfishing, the number of coral eating predators, such as snails, worms and damselfishes have proliferated. The only practical solution on the horizon for the present crisis is the restoration of the natural predator/prey relationships through the establishment of a series of Caribbean-wide no-harvest zones.

The Long-spined Urchin, *Diadema antillarum,* an important herbivore that plays a significant roll in controlling aggressive algae growth, has failed to recover substantially from a mysterious disease that decimated its populations throughout the Caribbean in 1983. In its absence coral reefs have suffered greatly from an explosion of coral-competing macroalgae, which prevents the settlement and survival of coral larvae and also encroaches on established stony corals. It has been documented that coral colonies surrounded by thick algal mats are more susceptible to disease. Recent experiments in Puerto Rico suggest that a reintroduction of sea urchins may reduce Black-band Disease infections.

Limited efforts to treat corals affected by certain diseases have proven highly successful for colonies affected by Black-band Disease. The Black-bands are aspirated from the colony with a vacuum and the waste material collected to prevent its spread to surrounding corals. Underwater putty is then applied to act as a barrier between the affected area and healthy tissue. This technique has been attempted with White Plague and Yellow-blotch Disease with moderate success, but underwater putty is relatively expensive and only a limited number of corals can be realistically treated in this manner. Shading colonies affected with Black-band Disease also significantly reduces the disease.

While treatments for diseases represent a short-term solution, they can only be conducted on a small scale and are only effective for specific diseases. Region-wide protection of corals from disease organisms will require a more significant effort. Greatly expanded field monitoring to assess the health of coral reefs and additional laboratory studies to better understand the nature of coral diseases are urgently needed.

Another strategy involves the development of restoration technologies to enhance the survival of coral fragments, promote settlement and recruitment of coral larvae, and to culture small branches for eventual reintroduction to degraded areas. Because of the large losses sustained by Elkhorn Coral and Staghorn Coral, NOAA/ National Marine Fisheries Service added these species to the Candidate Species List of the Endangered Species Act (ESA) in June, 1999. While candidate species status does not provide legal protection, a full ESA listing would prevent harmful activities such as dredging in areas near U.S. coral reefs and provide better protection for the listed corals and the coral reef environment overall. Further, an ESA listing requires the development and implementation of a recovery program in an attempt to restore the species to their former abundance.

Strategies to mitigate land-based threats are paramount for addressing coral diseases. Rivers, coastal run-off and sewage discharge increase the pollutants that enter the coral reef environment, stressing the corals and making them more likely to become diseased. While many people think that run-off and discharge into the ocean are coastal problems, impacts originating far inland have a cumulative effect on the health of coral reefs.

NOAA/NMFS, in collaboration with the United Nations Environmental Program's World Conservation Monitoring Center, has recently established a global coral disease database. This project, which can be viewed at *www.unep-wcmc.org/marine/coraldis/home.htm,* links coral disease records to existing coral reef maps, and is helping scientists and managers better understand the distribution of diseases and their linkage with human impact. Recreational divers can contribute information to the database using the online data form and the information in this chapter as a tool to assist in the identification of diseases. Your help in identifying locations of disease outbreaks can further help in the development of solutions to mitigate effects associated with the recent emergence of coral diseases.

The Reproduction and Growth of Stony Corals

To compete successfully in a reef community, corals need to increase both in numbers and in size. Stony corals are notable in the animal kingdom for their complex suite of reproductive strategies both sexual and asexual. Sexual reproduction creates genetically new individuals from the combination of male and female genes produced by different parental colonies. This process is called genetic recombination. Although differences resulting from the shuffling of genes from one generation to the next may be small, the implications can be great over time. New combinations and slight variations over many generations can lead to adaptations that may provide resistance or increased susceptibility to diseases or stresses such as increased temperatures and pollution. Colonies grow larger by adding new polyps through asexual reproduction: the development of genetically identical clones without the union of male and female gametes.

Understanding sexual reproduction of corals is a bit tricky because some coral species have separate male and female colonies whereas other corals are hermaphroditic, producing both eggs and sperm in the same colony. In addition, the fertilization of eggs, which develop into tiny free-living offspring known as **planula larvae,** can take place inside a colony or outside in open water. Corals that develop planula larvae internally are called **brooders;** species that release eggs, sperm or both into the water column are known as **broadcast spawners.**

Most large, reef-building coral species release millions of gametes once a year in precisely synchronized mass-spawning events. Broadcast spawning allows the stationary animals to mix genetically and to disperse offspring over great distances. Such a copious delivery system is also believed to maximize the chances of fertilization and, at the same time, overwhelm predators with more food than they can possibly consume. The exact cues triggering the annual phenomenon remain unclear. The triggering of the spawn is believed to be linked to water temperatures as well as the lunar, tidal and the 24-hour light cycle.

A few broadcast spawners, known as gonochoric species, have separate male and female colonies, and, depending on their sex, either release sperm or eggs, which, with luck, will cross-fertilize somewhere in the vast water column. Most broadcast spawners, however, are hermaphrodites (both sexes occurring in each individual coral polyp). Such polyps once a year package both sperm and eggs into neat little pink gamete bundles that are expelled to the caprice of the currents when a biological clock strikes.

Fertilization, which is possibly aided by sperm attractants, produces planulae larvae that are able to swim on their own by day two. Once, in the grasp of tides and currents, the tiny larval coral embarks on a grand voyage that can last for months and carry it hundreds of miles from its point of origin. If the speck of life somehow survives the ever-hungry mouths of plankton-picking and filter-feeding invertebrates and fishes, it will one day mysteriously sense to settle on hard substrate in clear shallow water and begin producing a tiny calcium skeleton – the possible genesis of a coral colony that could live for hundreds of years.

In the Caribbean, the magical night of the largest mass coral spawn typically occurs in the evening eight days after the full moon of August when the star coral complex reproduces. If the full moon occurs early in the month, it is possible that a split spawning occurs: the first in August and again in September.

On the night of the mass coral spawn Giant Star Coral, *Montastraea cavernosa*, discharges stream of smoke-like gametes just after dusk; Boulder Star Coral, *M. franksi*, releases egg/sperm bundles around 9:30 p.m.; Lobed Star Coral, *M. annularis* and Mountainous Star Coral between 10:30 and 11 p.m. Several species of brain corals and *Acropora* (Staghorn and Elkhorn Corals) take place a few days before.

Giant Star Coral releasing smoke-like gametes.

Maze Coral releasing smoke-like gametes.

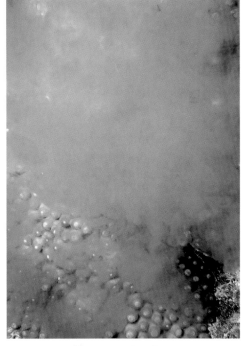

Heavy gamete release obscures Giant Star Coral colony.

Coral Reproduction

Boulder Star Coral polyps swollen with gamete bundles.

Boulder Star Coral polyps in various stages of gamete bundles release.

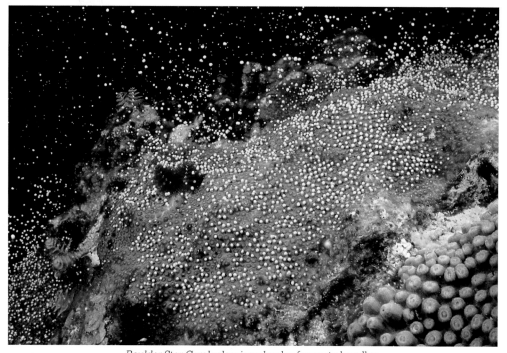

Boulder Star Coral releasing clouds of gamete bundles.

Symmetrical Brain Coral polyps swollen with gamete bundles. Note brittle star feeding on emerging gamete bundles.

Detail of Symmetrical Brain Coral polyps releasing gamete bundles.

Butterflyfishes and brittle starfish feeding on gamete bundles of Symmetrical Brain Coral release.

Coral Reproduction

Planula larvae can remain viable for weeks or months while riding the currents in the open water. Soon after settling to the sea floor the specks of life begin secreting a calcium carbonate covering. Soon they are ready to produce new polyps through asexual reproduction: the first step in becoming a colony. New polyps, depending on the species of coral, either erupt between or "bud" from established polyps, a process called extratentacular budding (literally, between tentacles) or, as the polyp grows, it divides or splits-off one or more new polyps, a process called **fission** (intratentacular budding).

Most of the Caribbean's branching and mound-building corals add new corallites through **budding.** If closely observed, new, smaller corallites can be seen emerging from the base of established corallites on branching corals and erupting between older corallites on the surface mound-building colonies.

Orange Solitary Coral budding a new polyp from the base of the corallite. [below left]
Massive Starlet Coral polyps construct pit-like corallites. The tiny pits between larger corallites are new polyps erupting. [below right]
Tube Coral buds numerous tiny new polyps around larger established corallites. [bottom left]
Staghorn Coral increases the length of branches by budding tiny terminal polyps around their bases. [bottom right]

Brain corals, cactus corals, sheet corals and others that have polyps associated with ridges or grooves generally add new polyps through **fission.** Polyps anywhere along a ridge can replicate in this manner, providing great variation in a colony's shape or ridge pattern. This process can be easily observed in Spiny Flower Coral, *Mussa angulosa,* and Elliptical Star Coral, *Dichocoenia stokesii.*

Large polyp of Spiny Flower Coral divides and splits off three new polyps. [below left]
Smooth Flower Coral polyps dividing into two polyps. [below right]
Knobby Cactus Coral polyp dividing into two polyps. [bottom left]
Golfball Coral polyps lengthen and then fold inward to divide into two polyps; note the long oval corallite starting to fold inward and the two small side-by-side recently divided polyps. [bottom right]

Coral Reproduction

New coral colonies also form by **fragmentation** when pieces of colonies break off due to strong currents, storms, anchor damage, boat grounding, careless divers, or as the result of bio-erosions or predators. If the fragments are of sufficient size and settle on appropriate substrate, they establish distinct new colonies that are genetically identical to the parental colonies. Numerous Caribbean corals are known to reproduce by fragmentation, including branching and pillar and many of the mound-building and boulder corals. It is likely that fragmentation is an important mode of colony replication for many other species.

The advantages of fragmentation over sexual reproduction include increased recruitment rates and likelihood of success, as well as increased abundance and distribution of species in the reef area. A potential disadvantage is minimized genetic diversity. Clonemates will have the same susceptibility to disease or bleaching events, increasing the chance that large numbers of colonies will be affected by adverse conditions.

Broken pieces of Staghorn Coral begin attachment to hard substrate and start upward branching growth regenerating new colonies. Fragmentation is this species primary means of new colony formation. [below]
Pillar Coral columns, probably broken of by the force of large storm waves, regenerate new colonies. [bottom]

INDEX

PERSONAL RECORD OF CORAL SIGHTINGS

1. FIRE & LACE CORALS

No.	Name	Page	Date	Location
	Branching Fire Coral *Millepora alcicornis*	17		
	Blade Fire Coral *Millepora complanata*	19		
	Box Fire Coral *Millepora squarrosa*	19		
	Rose Lace Coral *Stylaster roseus*	21		

2. GORGONIANS, TELESTACEANS & SOFT CORALS

	Name	Page	Date	Location
	Corky Sea Finger *Briareum asbestinum*	27		
	Encrusting Gorgonian *Erythropodium caribaeorum*	29		
	Black Sea Rod *Plexaura homomalla*	29		
	Bent Sea Rod *Plexaura flexuosa*	31		
	Porous Sea Rods *Pseudoplexaura* spp.	33		
	Knobby Sea Rods *Eunicea* spp.	35		
	Swollen-knob Candelabrum *Eunicea mammosa*	35		
	Shelf-knob Sea Rod *Eunicea succinea*	37		
	Warty Sea Rod *Eunicea calyculata*	39		
	Doughnut Sea Rod *Eunicea fusca*	39		
	Slit-Pore Sea Rods *Plexaurella* spp.	41		
	Giant Slit-pore Sea Rod *Plexaurella nutans*	43		
	Spiny Sea Fan *Muricea muricata*	43		
	Long Spine Sea Fan *Muricea pinnata*	45		
	Orange Spiny Sea Rod *Muricea elongata*	47		
	Delicate Spiny Sea Rod *Muricea laxa*	47		
	Rough Sea Plume *Muriceopsis flavida*	49		
	Sea Plumes *Pseudopterogorgia* spp.	51		
	Slimy Sea Plume *Pseudopterogorgia americana*	51		
	Bipinnate Sea Plume *Pseudopterogorgia bipinnata*	53		
	Yellow Sea Whip *Pterogorgia citrina*	53		
	Grooved-blade Sea Whip *Pterogorgia guadalupensis*	55		

No.	Name	Page	Date	Location
	Angular Sea Whip *Pterogorgia anceps*	57		
	Common Sea Fan *Gorgonia ventalina*	57		
	Venus Sea Fan *Gorgonia flabellum*	59		
	Wide-mesh Sea Fan *Gorgonia mariae*	61		
	Deepwater Sea Fan *Iciligorgia schrammi*	61		
	Colorful Sea Rod *Diodogorgia nodulifera*	63		
	Brilliant Sea Fingers *Titanideum frauenfeldii*	65		
	Red Polyp Octocoral *Swiftia exserta*	65		
	Devil's Sea Whip *Ellisella barbadensis*	67		
	Long Sea Whip *Ellisella elongata*	69		
	Orange Deep Water Fan *Nicella goreaui*	69		
	Bushy Sea Whip *Nicella schmitti*	71		
	Colorful Sea Whip *Leptogorgia virgulata*	73		
	Regal Sea Fan *Leptogorgia hebes*	75		
	Carmine Sea Spray *Leptogorgia miniata*	75		
	Pinnate Spiny Sea Fan *Muricea pendula*	77		
	White Eye Sea Spray *Thesea nivea*	79		
	Golden Sea Spray *Heterogorgia uatumani*	81		
	Rigid Red Telesto *Stereotelesto corallina*	81		
	White Telesto *Carijoa riisei*	83		
	Orange Telesto *Telesto fruticulosa*	83		
	Pastel Soft Coral *Neospongodes portoricensis*	85		

3. STONY CORALS

No.	Name	Page	Date	Location
	Staghorn Coral *Acropora cervicornis*	91		
	Fused Staghorn *Acropora prolifera*	91		
	Elkhorn Coral *Acropora palmata*	93		
	Finger Coral *Porites porites*	95		
	Pillar Coral *Dendrogyra cylindrus*	97		

No.	Name	Page	Date	Location
	Tube Coral *Cladocora arbuscula*	99		
	Robust Ivory Tree Coral *Oculina robusta*	99		
	Delicate Ivory Bush Coral *Oculina tenella*	101		
	Diffuse Ivory Bush Coral *Oculina diffusa*	101		
	Large Ivory Coral *Oculina varicosa*	103		
	Yellow Pencil Coral *Madracis mirabilis*	103		
	Eight-ray Finger Coral *Madracis formosa*	105		
	Ten-ray Star Coral *Madracis decactis*	107		
	Six-ray Star Coral *Madracis senaria*	107		
	Star Coral *Madracis pharensis*	109		
	Blue Crust Coral *Porites branneri*	109		
	Blushing Star Coral *Stephanocoenia intersepta*	111		
	Boulder Star Coral *Montastraea annularis*	113		
	Great Star Coral *Montastraea cavernosa*	115		
	Smooth Star Coral *Solenastrea bournoni*	117		
	Knobby Star Coral *Solenastrea hyades*	117		
	Elliptical Star Coral *Dichocoenia stokesi*	119		
	Golfball Coral *Favia fragum*	121		
	Mustard Hill Coral *Porites astreoides*	121		
	Massive Starlet Coral *Siderastrea siderea*	123		
	Lesser Starlet Coral *Siderastrea radians*	123		
	Symmetrical Brain Coral *Diploria strigosa*	125		
	Knobby Brain Coral *Diploria clivosa*	125		
	Grooved Brain Coral *Diploria labyrinthiformis*	127		
	Maze Coral *Meandrina meandrites*	129		
	Rose Coral *Manicina areolata*	131		
	Boulder Brain Coral *Colpophyllia natans*	133		
	Honeycomb Plate Coral *Porites colonensis*	135		
	Sunray Lettuce Coral *Helioseris cucullata*	135		

No.	Name	Page	Date	Location
	Fragile Saucer Coral *Agaricia fragilis*	137		
	Whitestar Sheet Coral *Agaricia lamarcki*	139		
	Dimpled Sheet Coral *Agaricia grahamae*	141		
	Scroll Coral *Agaricia undata*	141		
	Lettuce Coral *Agaricia agaricites*	145		
	Low Relief Lettuce Coral *Agaricia humilis*	147		
	Thin Leaf Lettuce Coral *Agaricia tenuifolia*	147		
	Ridged Cactus Coral *Mycetophyllia lamarckiana*	149		
	Knobby Cactus Coral *Mycetophyllia aliciae*	151		
	Rough Cactus Coral *Mycetophyllia ferox*	151		
	Ridgeless Cactus Coral *Mycetophyllia reesi*	153		
	Sinuous Cactus Coral *Isophyllia sinuosa*	155		
	Rough Star Coral *Isophyllastrea rigida*	155		
	Artichoke Coral *Scolymia cubensis*	157		
	Solitary Disk Coral *Scolymia wellsi*	157		
	Atlantic Mushroom Coral *Scolymia lacera*	159		
	Spiny Flower Coral *Mussa angulosa*	161		
	Baroque Cave Coral *Thalamophyllia riisei*	161		
	Smooth Flower Coral *Eusmilia fastigiata*	163		
	Orange Cup Coral *Tubastraea coccinea*	165		
	Porous Cup Coral *Balanophyllia floridana*	167		
	Colorful Cave Coral *Rhizopsammia goesi*	167		
	Speckled Cup Coral *Rhizosmilia maculata*	169		
	Lesser Speckled Cup Coral *Colangia immersa*	169		
	Cryptic Cave Coral *Colangia jamaicaensis*	171		
	Hidden Cup Coral *Phyllangia americana americana*	171		
	Dwarf Cup Coral *Astrangia solitaria*	173		
	Twotone Cup Coral *Phacelocyathus flos*	175		
	Ornate Cup Coral *Coenocyathus humanni*	175		

4. BLACK CORALS

No.	Name	Page	Date	Location
	Button Cup Coral *Coenocyathus caribbeana*	175		
	Bushy Black Coral *Antipathes n. sp.*	179		
	Feather Black Coral *Antipathes pennacea*	179		
	Orange Sea Fan Black Coral *Antipathes gracilis*	181		
	Gray Sea Fan Black Coral *Antipathes atlantica*	183		
	Hair Net Black Coral *Antipathes lenta*	183		
	Scraggly Black Coral *Antipathes n. sp.*	185		
	Bottle-brush Bush Black Coral *Antipathes hirta*	185		
	Scraggly Bottle-brush Black Coral *Antipathes barbadensis*	185		
	Bottle-brush Black Coral *Antipathes tanacetum*	187		
	Wire Coral *Cirrhipathes (Stichopathes) leutkeni*	187		

NOTES